Taking Conversations from

DIFFICULT
to
DOABLE

3 Models to Master
Tough Conversations

by Lynne Cunningham, MPA

Published by:
Fire Starter Publishing
350 W. Cedar Street, Suite 300
Pensacola, FL 32502
Phone: 866-354-3473
Fax: 850-332-5117
www.firestarterpublishing.com

ISBN: 978-1-622-18024-0

Library of Congress Control Number: 2015959140

Printed in the United States of America

A special thank-you to all of the leaders who have participated in my Three Models leadership development institutes and learned the importance of having these tough conversations. You articulated the need and served as the motivation for this book.

In memoriam, I express thanks to Beth Keane, who was the inspiration behind the Impact Message model. In living, she taught so many of us so much. In dying, she taught us courage and humility. Beth will always be remembered for her authenticity of practicing these communication techniques, her infectious laugh, and her ability to make a connection with everyone she met due to her warmth and sincerity.

As always, thank you to my husband, Glen, who has taught me how to trust and to love.

TABLE OF CONTENTS

FOREWORD

Over the years we've developed, gathered, and refined great tips for more effective communication. From rounding to AIDET® to dozens of other evidence-based practices, Studer Group® has become known for our practical, straight-forward ideas to improve communications with patients, coworkers, and physicians. Since the late '90s, our coaches have helped hundreds of healthcare organizations, and hundreds of thousands of leaders and physicians, adopt these principles. Lynne Cunningham is one of our very best at teaching people how to, as the title reads, make the difficult conversations doable.

In this book, Lynne has gathered the best of our communication practices into an easy-to-read guide that you'll reference for years to come. She puts a fresh twist on timeless concepts, interjecting her personal stories and those from the road to make the points hit home. And she has some stories! Her career has given her a unique, up-close view of the communication struggles and victories across just about every type of healthcare delivery organization. Lynne's by far the best-read person I know. She reads voraciously, sending out summaries of many of her healthcare and business books to hundreds of leaders across healthcare, and you'll see that she's paid attention to all of those authors through her easy-to-read style and approach.

Personally, this is a book I'm glad Lynne took the time to write. You'll see in her Dedication that Beth Keane was a major influence on this content and on Lynne personally. And it's no different for me. Like Lynne, Beth was a wonderful communicator who taught me much of what I know and get to pass along to others. Writing all of this down is a way to ensure that her purpose lives on for years to come.

At Studer Group we're grateful to the men and women who commit to improving their own skills, who take time to thank others who are doing it right, and who don't miss the opportunity to coach those who can do better. It's what our patients and families deserve. And it's humbling to know that you're taking the time to read this book to move your own communication prowess and confidence to the next level. Thank you for your commitment to making healthcare better.

—Craig E. Deao, MHA

INTRODUCTION

After spiders, snakes, and public speaking, one of our biggest fears is having tough conversations with other people. It doesn't matter if the conversation needs to occur with a colleague, friend, spouse, or child; we all shy away from these critical communications. Often, we're particularly reluctant to bring up sensitive topics with coworkers, team members, supervisors, and other individuals in the workplace. Why?

- We don't believe we possess the skills to have the conversation in a professional manner.

- The behavior has been going on a long time and we've never said anything before.

- The employee's annual performance review is coming up and we think it will just be easier to wait for that opportunity to discuss the offending behavior.

- The other person gets emotional anytime you make suggestions on how to do something differently.

- The person's best friend (or neighbor, sister, fellow church member—you get the picture) is a prominent physician, board member, executive team member, etc.

- We're afraid of the other person because they have a reputation for reacting negatively, pouting, or taking their displeasure out on other employees (or patients) when they are corrected or coached.

Underlying all of these reasons for our hesitancy is the fact that we often don't understand the seriousness of biting the bullet and having the conversation. This book will give you tools to overcome all of the obstacles listed above, but I'd like to address the *why* behind difficult conversations right here, up front: Your willingness and ability to constructively address undesirable behaviors can make or break your organization's ability to meet its goals and provide top-quality care to patients (or top-quality service to customers).

In the *Harvard Business Review*, Monique Valcour writes:

Giving developmental feedback that sparks growth is a critical challenge to master, because it can make the difference between an employee who contributes powerfully and positively to the organization and one who feels diminished by the organization and contributes far less. A single conversation can switch an employee on—or shut her down. A true developmental leader sees the raw material for brilliance in every employee and creates the conditions to let it shine, even when the challenge is tough.[1]

The point is, successfully conducting difficult conversations is not a nice-to-have skill for leaders; it's a must-have skill. It is critical that you be able to recognize detrimental actions and behaviors, compassionately bring them to the other person's attention, and then coach that employee toward positive change.

There is one more thing I want to make clear at the beginning of this book: Please don't confuse "difficult conversations" with lectures, "talking-tos," or "dressing-downs." The point of the conversational models I share in this book is not to punish, embarrass, or put an employee "in their place." In fact—as we'll discuss—approaching a conversation with this intent will be counterproductive. In her *Harvard Business Review* article, Monique Valcour writes that effective coaching contains the following three elements:

1. *An intention to help the employee grow, rather than to show him he was wrong. The feedback should increase, not drain, the employee's motivation and resources for change…*

2. *Openness on the part of the feedback giver, which is essential to creating a high-quality connection that facilitates change. If you start off feeling uncomfortable and self-protective, your employee will match that energy, and you'll each leave the conversation frustrated with the other person.*

3. *Inviting the employee into the problem-solving process. You can ask questions such as: What ideas do you have? What are you taking away from this conversation? What steps will you take, by when, and how will I know?*[2]

In other words, *your* attitude and approach will set the tone for—and determine the outcome of—the conversation. These interactions are as much about you as they are the other person. That's why it's so important to learn about and practice conducting difficult conversations.

As I travel across the country and talk to leaders about how to master tough conversations, I'm often asked:

- How do you know when you need to have the conversation?

- How do you prepare?

- What do you say?

- How do you recover if you lose control?

- Can you have a tough conversation with a physician, peer, or even your boss?

- What if you need to have a tough conversation with a high performer?

The list goes on and on. No matter how many times I work with an organization, they want more practice and education on how to master tough conversations.

Much has been written about how to have tough conversations. As someone who has read dozens of business books each year for the past 25 years, I feel qualified to say that many existing books on this subject are complicated and ponderous. I think leaders are looking for quick tips and a clear (or clearer) decision-making structure to determine how to approach and execute a conversation with a peer, direct report, boss, or physician when actions are not appropriate.

That's my goal with this short book. It answers common questions like, *Why is it important to have these tough conversations? What happens when we ignore the situations? How can we create a win-win? What do we do if the behavior doesn't change?*

To help you apply theory to reality, we'll cover Studer Group's three models for conducting difficult conversations: the **Stub Your Toe Conversation**, the **Impact Message**, and the **Low Performer Conversation**. These three models for tough conversations need to become part of every leader's toolkit. The key is to learn about the models, practice them, and pick the appropriate model for each individual situation.

I've pulled together a curriculum to help leaders understand how and when to use each model. I have also included a large number of examples (many of which I have gathered from actual organizations) that illustrate how to structure tough conversations to ensure the greatest likelihood of success.

Additionally, you'll find several chapters devoted to tools that support difficult conversations and several more chapters that examine common barriers to conducting tough conversations (and how to overcome them).

Although my background is in healthcare, these tools, tips, and many of the sample conversations can easily translate into other industries. Just as our goal in healthcare is to provide the highest quality care to our patients, non-healthcare companies' and nonprofits' ultimate goal is to serve and satisfy the customer. As we pursue this purpose, difficult conversations are sometimes necessary to coach employees and shift their behavior.

What You Won't Find in This Book

There are some things this book is not going to do. If you listen to National Public Radio on the weekend, you're probably familiar with Click and Clack, the *Car Talk* guys (with tribute to Tom Magliozzi, *Car Talk* co-host who died in November 2014). They dish out equal parts of advice on how to deal with a car problem and advice on how to solve your marital problems! This book is strictly about work-related tough conversations—no marital advice. I don't have that kind of experience as I've been married to the same guy for over 40 years.

I tell audiences across the country that if you "keep the face of the patient in front of you, you'll do the right thing and have the tough conversation." Whether it's the face of the patient or the face of the customer in another industry, that's why this skill set is critical. Our patients and customers are depending on us, but so are our employees who don't want to watch others break the rules and get away with it—over and over and over.

Let's get started!

PART ONE:

THE SKILLS NEEDED TO HAVE EFFECTIVE DIFFICULT CONVERSATIONS

Chapter One:

It All Starts with
Building Trust

Tough conversations—more specifically, tough conversations with successful outcomes—don't just happen. They're built on an important framework of interlocking prerequisites, the first of which is *trust*. For trust to exist, two people must have a positive relationship. And for a positive relationship to be in place, solid communications must be present.

To start, I'd like to share a story that demonstrates how trust and positive relationships can help people overcome obstacles and achieve great things:

I am afraid of heights. I think maybe I've always been afraid of heights. I don't really know why. I don't even like to climb up on that three-step stool in the kitchen to remove something from a tall cabinet. My husband of over 40 years is very patient with me, often guiding me, holding my hand, and coaching me along on a hike or when flying. Glen knows that when I say, "Enough!" I usually mean it. My good friends, and anyone who has hiked or skied with me, all know I'm afraid of heights, too.

My husband and I were hiking in Yosemite with a group of friends several years ago. We had reservations to climb Half Dome one day and everyone was pretty excited—except me. I had graciously volunteered to stay in the camp and keep critters away from our gear while the group climbed Half Dome to see the sunrise. The plan was solid but…there had been bears in the camp during the night. I didn't want to be alone if they returned. So when the alarm went off at 3:30 a.m., I got up, too. My husband said, "Hike only as far as you are comfortable, bring a book, and wait for us."

This sounded like a good plan to me. We started hiking, with Glen coaxing me along all the way. Since it was still dark, our only light was the tiny head lamps we each wore. When we got to the base of "the climb," Glen encouraged me to give it a try—and I did. It was still dark when I reached the summit with Glen behind me all the way, coaching and encouraging. Our friends cheered when they saw me, as they knew what an accomplishment this was for me.

The sunrise was incredible on top of the world. Our group had breakfast, and then it was time to head back down. That's when I got scared. It was light, and I could see! I might still be on top of Half Dome if a friend hadn't expertly coached me down. He instructed me to look into the granite face as I descended so I couldn't see the height, instead of looking out to enjoy what I'm told was a glorious view. I made it down!

That day I accomplished something I never thought I'd be able to do—and it was entirely because of a loving husband and kind friends who coached and encouraged me. I've climbed Half Dome once. I have the pictures. I got the t-shirt. I don't need to do it again. But I'm awfully glad I had strong relationships and trusted these folks. That was a special day.

I think you get the point. Trusting relationships allow us to overcome obstacles, leave our limitations in the dust, and in general grow as human beings. Difficult conversations may be the catalyst for that growth, but it's trust that allows the "talker" to broach the subject and the "listener" to hear and accept what is said.

Trust Makes All the Difference

Be honest: If your supervisor pulled you aside and told you that your performance needed to change—but you did not believe that your supervisor cared about your feelings or your future—what would your reaction be? You'd probably feel angry, defensive, embarrassed, and upset. None of these emotions would help you thoughtfully consider your supervisor's suggestion. You might even be inclined to ignore your supervisor, start an argument, or try to pass responsibility to someone else.

Now, imagine that after acknowledging your contributions and emphasizing how important your work is to the organization, your supervisor suggests a way for you to improve your performance. You feel confident that your supervisor wants you to succeed, has your best interests at heart, and will continue to support you. You are able to calmly consider your supervisor's suggestion, and are much more likely to willingly implement the suggested behavior.

What was the difference? In Scenario Two, you trusted your supervisor. You felt safe in the knowledge that they were trying to help, not hurt, you. That's the power of trust. Trust sparks growth. Without it, a difficult conversation is "just" a reprimand.

Rounding: A Tool to Help You Build Trust and Relationships

Mutual trust and positive relationships don't just appear out of thin air—they must be earned and then consistently nurtured. I'm going to share several suggestions to help you build trust and nurture strong relationships in your organization. The first method we'll look at is rounding. Rounding is an evidence-based tactic that will enable you to build relationships and form a solid communications foundation with your team.

If you're familiar with Studer Group®, you already know that we are huge proponents of rounding. If you're not, you may think it's something only doctors and nurses do with patients. That's not true. Increasingly, rounding is being adapted in all types of healthcare organizations and by other industries and businesses seeking to positively impact employee engagement and customer satisfaction.

Basically, when leaders round on employees, it's more than just a "by the way" conversation in the hall. It's more purposeful and deliberate than that. We are rounding *for outcomes*, which means we're asking very specific questions and seeking to accomplish very specific things. We are seeking to build relationships, to harvest "wins," to identify process improvement areas, and to make sure people have everything they need to do their jobs.

Notice the first item in that list. Whether we are rounding on our staff members, on internal customers, or on our patients, we are building positive relationships. We're showing that we (and by extension our organizations) are predictable, structured, and dependable. Rounding lets us and those we serve know what to expect. All of this serves to build trust. And when colleagues, patients, or customers trust us to do our jobs and care for their needs, they will freely tell us what's working well and where we have opportunities for improvement. They will also be more receptive to listening and making changes when difficult conversations are necessary.

Implementing Rounding in Your Organization

When Studer Group coaches teach a new partner organization about rounding, we recommend that they follow several key steps. First, we teach the leaders about rounding (the *why* behind it) and have them practice it with each other, so they become familiar with asking the questions (which we'll discuss soon) and taking notes. Then we encourage them to tell staff about rounding at a team meeting so it's not a surprise when it is implemented. Here are a few points to keep in mind when you introduce rounding to your team:

- Explain that rounding is an Evidence-Based Leadership[SM] tactic to facilitate communication with each team member, enable individuals to provide input and feedback, and create a consistent culture in the work unit and organization.

- Establish the expectation that rounding will happen monthly and individually with each employee, and that the conversation will take about 5-7 minutes.

- Make it clear that rounding is not a substitute for other types of formal meetings or problem solving sessions, but is a consistent method for building relationships and ensuring each individual's voice is heard.

Finally, leaders start rounding on each direct report on a monthly basis. They keep a log of what they hear and report their findings to their one-up during a monthly meeting.

How Frequently Should Leaders Round?

The ideal is for leaders to round on all of their direct reports each month. Since the number one factor in an employee's decision to stay in or leave a job is their immediate supervisor, rounding is the best tool a leader has to strengthen that bond. If a leader has 40 or fewer direct reports, that means a leader would, on average, round on two employees each day. However, if a leader has more than 40 direct reports, then a less frequent schedule is recommended. Essentially, it is about finding the right balance. If you can't round on everyone in one month, try to break them up into two months. This way, all staff will have been rounded on at least every other month. Essentially, it's about finding the balance that works best for leaders and builds strong relationships with their teams.

The rounding questions we initially teach leaders are based on the Gallup organization's Q^{12} employee engagement survey questions (so they are evidence-based). See Figure 1.1:

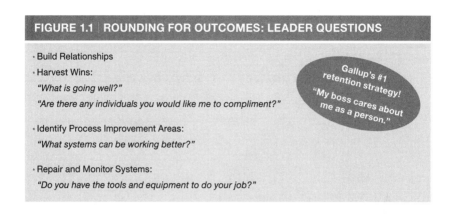

FIGURE 1.1 ROUNDING FOR OUTCOMES: LEADER QUESTIONS

- Build Relationships
- Harvest Wins:
  "What is going well?"
  "Are there any individuals you would like me to compliment?"
- Identify Process Improvement Areas:
  "What systems can be working better?"
- Repair and Monitor Systems:
  "Do you have the tools and equipment to do your job?"

Gallup's #1 retention strategy! "My boss cares about me as a person."

The first month a leader starts rounding, employees may be skeptical about the process, or they may not feel comfortable sharing the real issues they have. By assuring employees that follow-up will happen—and then making sure it does—the leader keeps the lines of communication open and begins the important process of building trust.

After a few months, as leaders become proficient with the questions and employees are comfortable with the conversation, many ask how they can "change up" what they ask during rounding. I recommend that you look at rounding as a series of "buckets." Focus on filling each of the following buckets as you ask questions that align with your organization's goals and initiatives:

- **The "What's Working Well" bucket.** First, ask, "What's working well?" When you begin the conversation by talking about good things in the organization and with the employee's job, you start rounding off on a positive note.

- **The "Reward and Recognition" bucket.** Learn how you can foster teamwork by recognizing and complimenting others who have been supportive of the employee.

- **The "Opportunities for Improvement" bucket.** Ask about improvement opportunities the employee sees and genuinely listen to their concerns and suggestions.

For instance, if you're in the middle of a software conversion or a Standards of Behavior rollout (See Chapter 8), you might figure out which "bucket" these issues best fit into and adjust the questions accordingly:

- Instead of a general, "What's working well?" ask, "What has worked well in the last week?" or, "What was working well yesterday?" or, "What's working well with our new software conversion?" You get the picture.

- For reward and recognition, ask something about your Standards of Behavior. For instance, "I'd like to write thank-you notes this month to employees who best exemplify our Standard of Teamwork. Who's doing a great job in that area?"

- To identify opportunities for improvement, think about asking, "What one change would you like to make that could substantially improve our patients' satisfaction?" or, "What about the software conversion is a concern to you or is an area where you need more training?"

To ensure that rounding is as effective as possible, be sure to let your employees know in advance what questions you will be changing. Remember, while rounding is meant to strengthen relationships, it is still quite formulated and specific. Consistency is very, very important.

That said, as you become more comfortable with the basic rounding questions and with filling your "buckets," you will be able to let the conversation flow more naturally. It is fine to start the interaction by asking about something important to the employee (e.g., family, pets, sports, a recent vacation, etc.).

And one final tip: Close the conversation by asking about tools and equipment. It's fascinating how often this simple question gives employees the freedom to mention seemingly small needs that have become "burr under the saddle blanket" issues to them. (In my experience, many employees are initially reluctant to bring up resource issues that have been forcing them to come up with work-arounds.) Administrative employees may talk about having to search for and share a stapler. Kitchen workers might bring up the 16-slice toaster they've had for years and that now has frayed wires. Quickly addressing these concerns communicates to your team members that you are listening, are concerned about their safety and work area, and can be trusted to take action.

My former Studer Group colleague Lyn Ketelsen says, "Coaching is caring"—and she is absolutely right. And caring means *consistently* creating a culture in which people can do their best work and feel that their feedback is welcome. Rounding achieves that goal better than any other tactic I know—which is why I've singled it out and placed it at the beginning of this book. I hear great stories all over the country about employees who are initially skeptical of rounding, but who quickly come to appreciate the one-on-one time and use it as an opportunity to bring up issues they would be uncomfortable addressing in a group meeting.

Done consistently, rounding shows your team you care about their thoughts, opinions, and performance. In return, team members will show more trust and respect when it's necessary to have difficult conversations. This caring and trust will be woven into the very fabric of your organization's culture.

Other Tactics to Build Trust and Positive Relationships

Rounding is extremely effective, but it certainly isn't the only way to build a trusting relationship with team members and others in the organization. Here are more tactics that will help you develop positive, trusting relationships:

- **Look for opportunities to connect.** Connecting with a team member doesn't have to be pre-planned or time-consuming. When you see someone in passing, smile and greet them. If you have an opportunity, comment on something you know will be of interest to the other person. These brief interactions let team members know that you "see" them and care about them, even in the middle of a busy day.

- **Reward and recognize deserving employees.** For instance, if there's new clinical quality or patient satisfaction data that shows improvement, reward and recognize the individual or team. You might announce the improvement at the next team meeting or write a thank-you note to each individual. We'll talk more about reward and recognition programs in Chapter 7. For now, know that giving credit where credit is due shows people that they can trust you to deal appropriately with the situation—whether it's a win or an opportunity for improvement.

- **Get to know employees outside of their professional roles.** The strongest professional connections are augmented with non-work-related ties. I have a simple, low-tech exercise I like to use in leadership development sessions to reinforce the notion that we all have lives outside of work. In small groups of about six, I ask everyone to share a non-work-related fact that others will likely not be aware of. Often these are employees who have worked together for years, but everyone always seems to be able to share a fact that surprises others. There's lots of laughter in the groups and a new realization that we can always learn more about people.

- **Encourage feedback and suggestions during daily huddles.** As a leader, you might set the agenda for daily huddles, but try not to dominate the conversation. Set aside a few minutes during which team members can highlight personal wins, share challenges, and request support. When everyone's voice is heard, mutual understanding and respect will grow.

- **Institute an open-door policy.** Often, employees are reluctant to offer suggestions or ask for support because they think their leader is "too busy." Yes, you may be *very* busy—but the benefits of having an open-door policy are worth the occasional interruptions. Let your team know that it's okay to stop in or call you when they need to. Tell them that if you are unavailable or can't answer, you'll touch base as soon as possible.

Note that communication—which is frequent, clear, sincere, and caring—is the foundation on which trust is built. In the next chapter, I'll discuss additional tactics to help you communicate accurately and effectively with your team and with others. Then you'll be ready to delve into the three models for mastering tough conversations.

CHAPTER TWO:

FOUR STEPS TO FACILITATE TOUGH CONVERSATIONS

W hether you need to have a tough conversation with an employee, colleague, or even your boss, there are four steps that will help you conduct the most successful dialogues.

1. Monitor Motives

2. Practice Presence

3. Clarify Expectations

4. Plan and Practice

Monitor Motives: Why Are You Having This Conversation?

First, let's look at Monitor Motives. This step involves examining why you need to have this tough conversation. What is your objective? What do you hope to accomplish?

I have found that if your organization's Standards of Behavior (see Chapter 8) and/or the patient (or other customer) are at the center of your motivations, you are on track to have a conversation that's respectful and productive. However, if you find that you are being driven primarily by anger, frustration, or another upsetting emotion, it's wise to pause and reexamine your intended course of action. Strong feelings like these can lead to a conversation in which the other person feels hurt, intimidated, or resentful—none of which are conducive to positive change. Remember, in most difficult conversations the goal is to *help* the other person. Ponder how you can create a win/win situation instead of one in which someone has to lose if you win.

My former colleague Beth Keane, to whom this book is dedicated, often talked about seeking to **complete** vs. **compete**. If you set up a scenario in which you are competing (for instance, trying to prove that you are right and the other person is wrong), some people will focus only on your tone and demeanor and not your message. They may also feel that it is unsafe to contribute to the conversation.

But when you enter a difficult conversation seeking more information (to complete your understanding of the situation), you're more likely to make better decisions. And with better decisions, you *and* the other person will be more likely to experience a successful outcome.

Let's consider an example. You've been hearing concerns that Dr. Jones's surgeries are consistently starting later than scheduled. How do you handle this situation? One option is to immediately initiate a counseling session about late start times, during which you imply that the issue is Dr. Jones's fault. This is an example of *competing* because you immediately blame Dr. Jones for the late start times. She will almost certainly respond defensively.

A second, wiser option is to begin by reviewing the data that documents the late start problem. Then, instead of accusing Dr. Jones of a personal problem with timeliness, ask why she thinks this has been happening. You may discover that she *has* been arriving on time, but the staff isn't ready or patients aren't being transported to the OR on a timely basis. This is an example of how seeking to *complete* helps ensure that focus remains on the problem and that it is addressed effectively and efficiently. Your tough conversations will go much more smoothly if you have your data prepared and ask your colleague for their views before jumping in with a solution.

Three Tips to Help You Complete, Not Compete

1. **Ease into it.** When you need to have a difficult conversation, it's often wise to "ease" into the tough topic. Talk about something positive or neutral so that the other person feels at ease and is not immediately put on the defensive. When people feel that they have been "attacked out of nowhere," they don't do their best listening or thinking—which will impair your efforts to "complete." At Studer Group®, we start our rounding by asking a relationship question like, *How was your weekend?* or, *Do you have new pictures of*

your grandchildren? or, *How about that ball team?* Questions like these can pave the way for a more productive, less contentious discussion.

2. **Say, *Yes, and...*instead of, *Yes, but...*** You'll find it's much more productive to have a tough conversation if you use the *Yes, and* syntax. Consider, "Suzy you're doing a great job learning that new task, BUT you'd finish more quickly if you changed the sequence of steps a little." The BUT diminishes the compliment with which the sentence started. Doesn't this sound more positive? "Suzy you're doing a great job learning that new task AND I think you'd be even more successful if you change the sequence of steps a little." When I am training leaders on how to master tough conversations, I remind them to keep the BUTs out of the conversation!

3. **Speak respectfully, especially when disagreeing.** We started this book by discussing why trust is essential if you want to successfully navigate difficult conversations. Trust and respect are closely tied, and both are necessary for "completion" to take place. The Joint Commission, the Institute for Safe Medication Practices, Alan Rosenstein, MD, and "Silence Kills: The Seven Crucial Conversations for Healthcare" all provide examples of the consequences when

trust and respect break down. (See appendix references.)

It's important to hold up the mirror during difficult conversations and, if necessary, adjust your behavior to create a safe, respectful environment. Let the Golden Rule be your guide. Ask yourself, *How would I feel if someone else talked to me this way? Would I be motivated to work toward resolution, or would I feel the need to defend myself?*

It can be especially tricky to keep the conversation respectful if you find that you must disagree with the other person. In this case, say, "I hear what you're saying. I'd like to respectfully disagree with your conclusion or the process you are suggesting." That's so much more positive than attacking, yelling, screaming, or stomping out of a meeting... or even simply sitting and seething.

These three tips will help you create a safe environment. That's important, because trust, respect, and safety are three legs of a stool that must be in balance to master tough conversations. If you can create a safe environment, you can talk with almost anyone about almost anything. People will feel safe when they think you respect them and you care about them.

As former Studer Group coach Lyn Ketelsen says, "Coaching is caring."

Practice Presence: How Well Are You Listening?

Let's move on to Practice Presence. In this context, when you are present, you are "in the moment," as the saying goes. You are physically occupying a space—but you are not dominating it. You are using your senses to learn as much as possible so that you can complete your understanding. (There's that phrase again!) In a nutshell, practicing presence means that you are giving the other person your full attention by looking them in the eye and listening to what they are saying.

Studies show that when we are at work, we spend:

- 9 percent of our time writing
- 16 percent of our time reading
- 30 percent of our time talking
- 45 percent of our time listening

That's right: We spend almost half of our time listening to other people. But have you ever thought about how effective a listener you are, or how you can improve your listening skills? For many of us, the answer is no. We all spent many hours in school learning about writing and reading, and maybe even public speaking. But few of us ever took a class to improve our listening skills. (In fact, only 2 percent have had formal educational experience with listening.) Wouldn't it make sense to put conscious effort into improving this skill that we use so often? Research certainly suggests that there's room for improvement:

- We usually recall just 50 percent of what was said immediately after speaking with someone.

- Over time we remember just 20 percent of what we hear.

If you are among the 98 percent of people who have never formally studied the art of listening, here are several lessons I've picked up over the course of my career. These lessons will help you become a more effective listener in any type of interaction, including the difficult conversation models we'll learn about in this book:

- **Think about what you're saying.** We touched on this idea earlier in the chapter when we talked about monitoring motives, but the idea bears repeating. We've all said (or even written) something we didn't really want to, then wished we could take back the words or e-mail. First, engage your brain. Then, engage your mouth.

- **Make listening your new default mode.** In other words, replace "waiting for my turn to talk" with "paying full attention to the other person." If you're thinking of a response or comeback while the other person is speaking, you'll miss half of what's being said, and misunderstandings are more likely to occur.

  When I think about listening instead of waiting for my turn to talk, I'm reminded of Thanksgiving dinner with my family. Many of us haven't seen each other for months, and everyone wants to share something. No one wants to wait for their turn, and multiple people try to talk at once. In the end, no one really communicates and we all feel frustrated.

Especially when you're having a difficult conversation, it's important to keep unnecessary frustration out of the interaction. Don't hesitate to say, "Thank you for sharing. Do you mind if I take a few moments to think about what you've said before I respond?"

- **Utilize the 12-second pause.** I learned about the 12-second pause from friends in Kansas who work at an organ procurement organization. (These are professionals who ask the families of dying patients for consent to recover organs and tissue that can be used in life-saving transplants.) If these professionals go straight from "I'm sorry your loved one is dying" to "Will you sign this consent?" they are much less likely to get a "yes." However, if they pause briefly (around 12 seconds) and allow the family member to process the situation, they are more likely to receive consent.

The information you'll be sharing in difficult conversations will often come as a surprise to the other person. When you strategically implement the 12-second pause, you will increase your chances of receiving a thoughtful, constructive response (as opposed to emotionally charged pushback).

Famous Quotes: It's All About the Ears

I have two favorite quotes that really reinforce the importance of listening:

- "There's a reason God gave us two ears and one mouth—so we can listen twice as much as we talk."

- That famous philosopher Henry Winkler (the Fonz from *Happy Days* and Eddie from *Royal Pains*) says, "The ear is the center of all relationships. Listening is the beginning and the end."

That said, the way in which we listen (and in fact, the way we practice presence) often depends on the setting of the conversation. Let's look at two of the most common types of interactions: in person and on the phone. The following graphs illustrate the aspects that contribute to face-to-face and telephone communications.

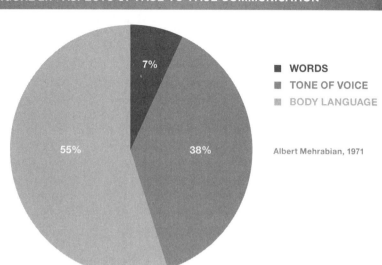

FIGURE 2.1 | ASPECTS OF FACE-TO-FACE COMMUNICATION

- WORDS
- TONE OF VOICE
- BODY LANGUAGE

7%

55%

38%

Albert Mehrabian, 1971

It's clear that body language has a significant impact on our face-to-face communications. We are all familiar with body language that communicates, "I want to talk, listen, and engage in this conversation." We open our arms, lean forward, lift up our heads and look at the person we're having a dialogue with. We also know that crossing arms, leaning back, and staring out the window communicate a message that says, "I don't really care what you are going to say; I'm going to disagree and do what I want to do anyway."

When you are having a tough conversation (or any conversation, for that matter), "listen" to what the other person's body language is telling you. If you sense disinterest or opposition, think about how you might change the tone of the discussion. (Hint: The "Three Tips to Help You Complete, Not Compete" I shared earlier in this chapter will probably help.) And, of course, be aware of what message your own body language is communicating. Pay special attention to eye contact, which conveys sincerity and demonstrates that you are giving the other person your undivided attention.

Another critical component of practicing presence in face-to-face conversations is eliminating distractions like cell phones, computers, and telephones. Multitasking indicates that you don't really respect the other person. (Even looking out the window can have this effect!) Again, it's difficult—maybe impossible—to create trust when there isn't respect, and you can't master a tough conversation successfully without trust.

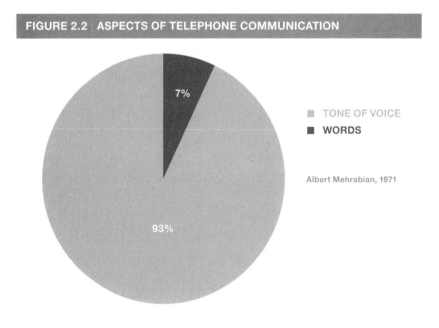

FIGURE 2.2 | ASPECTS OF TELEPHONE COMMUNICATION

7%

TONE OF VOICE

■ WORDS

Albert Mehrabian, 1971

93%

With telephone communications, body language, eye contact, and visible distractions don't come into play. Instead, it's the tone of our voice that speaks much louder than the actual words we use. Are you enthusiastic and encouraging? Or do you sound disinterested, distracted, impatient, or frustrated? If you are on the phone much of the day, put a mirror at your work station so you can "check your smile" as you speak. Your facial expression really does come through in your tone of voice.

Ultimately, it's always best to have tough conversations in person whenever possible. When you are face-to-face with the other person, you will have the benefit of seeing each other's body language as well as hearing the words that are said. Next best is on the phone—especially if you know the person well. When you have a preexisting positive relationship with the other person, you have a better chance of judging their non-verbal reaction to the conversation.

That said, with today's virtual companies and 24/7 operations, it's not always possible to set up a face-to-face meeting, or even a video conference. If you must have the tough conversation on the phone, be sure to prepare in advance, just as you would for an in-person discussion. Have your data in front of you, know the key points you want to make, and be prepared to listen.

Two Scenarios to Avoid

There are a couple of settings that make it nearly impossible to practice presence and that decrease the likelihood of a successful conversation. Avoid the following scenarios when you need to have a difficult conversation:

- If you need to coach someone on their behavior or correct a process, do so privately whenever possible. Remember "complete vs. compete"? Public criticism is a method of "competing" because it puts you in a position of power while causing the other person to feel ashamed or lose face.

- Although you may have itchy fingers, DON'T, under any circumstances, try to have a tough conversation via e-mail or text. It is very easy for tone, intent, emotion, and humor to be misconstrued. (Or, if you're distracted and you don't proofread the message carefully, you might say the wrong thing or send it to the wrong person!) Wait until you can see the other person face-to-face, or at least speak to them via telephone.

Clarify Expectations: Does the Other Person Understand What You Want?

Do you often feel frustrated because your instructions aren't followed or because standards are ignored? Why don't people do what you want them to do? It's common for leaders to assume that team members share their vision for what the task looks like when it is completed successfully. But in actuality, others often have different ideas and assumptions—which can lead to difficult conversations about performance, behavior, etc. This is why it is important to clarify expectations.

I may be a bit of a Pollyanna, but I don't really think people get up in the morning and say, "I'm going to work today at XYZ Hospital (or school or business) and I am going to do a terrible job." If someone isn't doing what you want them to do, first hold up the mirror and ask, "Have I clearly explained what a great job looks like and what will be accomplished when you complete the task?" If you can't immediately answer with a yes, maybe it's time to take a step back and explain the *why* for your request. Follow the *why* with *what* you want the individual to do and finally with *how* the task should be accomplished.

Start by using your best active listening skills. Ask the employee, coworker, or patient (or student, parent, or customer) to "teach back" what they think the task, assignment, or next step is before you move on. Make sure they understand the time frame necessary for success and know what specific outcome you are looking for.

Another tip is to ask, "What questions do you have?" instead of asking, "Do you have any questions?" after you have communicated your expectations. "What questions do you have?" implies that the other person *will* have questions to ask, and that it's okay to ask them. However, "Do you have any questions?" is often intimidating to the listener who fears judgment or a reprisal if they do ask a question, or if they ask the "wrong" question.

We see this all the time in the doctor's office. After providing a long, detailed explanation of test results or a diagnosis, the physician pauses briefly (sometimes with his hand on the door ready to leave) and says, "Do you have any questions?" As the patient, you don't even know where to start. Yes, of course you have questions! However, it's obvious that the doctor is in a hurry and you don't want to appear stupid so you say, "No. I'm fine." If the doctor were instead to ask, "What questions do you have?" while still seated and making eye contact, you would feel much more comfortable asking questions that would enable you to better understand the results and how to comply with the treatment regime.

You may need to start many difficult conversations by clarifying expectations. If a conversation has derailed and you are trying to resurrect trust, go back to this step to get the interaction back on track.

Plan and Practice: Do You Know What You Want to Accomplish and How to Do It?

Finally, we need to Plan and Practice. Each tough conversation should be approached as a unique opportunity to solve a problem, create a bond, or take performance to the next level. Before you begin the conversation, know where you want it to end. Carefully consider how you can create a win/win vs. a win/lose scenario.

Most of us are not so experienced at having tough conversations that we can avoid this step. Planning involves knowing what you want the conversation to accomplish and how you want it to end. The practice component can be role playing in your own head or inviting a colleague or friend to role play with you. There's no substitute for actually hearing the words you are planning to say before you use them in the real conversation. Plus, practicing beforehand reduces the chances that your mouth will "run away with you" in the heat of the moment.

It's helpful to frame the conversation before you engage a colleague or your HR partner in a practice session. Have your data at hand. Jot notes to help you include key points and write out specific words or phrases you want to use. All of this preparation will pay off with more professional conversations that have successful endings.

With planning, preparation, and practice, you won't have to look back on the difficult conversation and say,

- "I should have…"
- "I could have…"
- "I would have…"
- "I did have…"

There are many people who are ready to help you prepare for a tough conversation. Create the scenario you need to address and then practice the conversation with your boss, with a colleague, or with your HR partner. Once you have more practice and gain confidence, you can practice by yourself in front of the mirror or even with the cat or dog!

Practice Helps You Be Interested, Not Interesting

It's human nature to want to talk about ourselves. For instance, let's say you're talking to someone with a broken leg. After hearing about their accident, you tell the story of how you broke your leg years ago. That's being *interesting*, and there are many conversations where it's completely appropriate.

However, difficult conversations are *not* the time to be interesting. They are not about you or your experiences—they are meant to help the other person recognize and address a problematic behavior. When you practice these interactions beforehand, you are much less likely to become sidetracked and give into the temptation to be interesting.

When you put each of these steps into practice, you will be able to communicate more clearly, compassionately, and effectively. Remember, we classify difficult conversations as "difficult" for a reason. Don't make the mistake of approaching them in the same way as inherently positive interactions.

CHAPTER THREE:

Stub Your Toe
Conversations

Now that we've reviewed some strategies to help you prepare for and facilitate difficult conversations, let's examine how those conversations might be structured. As I mentioned in the Introduction, there are three models for tough conversations that should be in every leader's toolkit: the Stub Your Toe Conversation, the Impact Message, and the Low Performer Conversation.

The first, and least formal, model is the Stub Your Toe Conversation. This conversation can take place at any point in the workday—there is no need to schedule a meeting or sit down in an office. Any employee at any level can have a Stub Your Toe Conversation with another team member—initiating this model is not limited to leaders. (We'll discuss this in more detail later in the chapter.)

As taught by Studer Group®, the Stub Your Toe Conversation is used when you personally see or hear behavior that appears to be inconsistent with organizational policies, Standards of Behavior, or values. The key is to discuss the observed behavior as quickly as possible. This ensures that the other person is aware their behavior was observed and seemed inconsistent with organizational norms or values. If behavior that undermines the culture of respect and safety is not addressed in a timely fashion, the employee may perceive that it's okay to speak rudely to a colleague or patient, or to violate or "stretch" a policy. (As Studer Group speaker Liz Jazwiec says, "What you permit, you promote." We'll take a closer look at permit/promote in Chapter 10). And over time, an employee who continually fails to meet expectations without consequences negatively impacts the entire team's performance.

Gerald Hickson, MD, of Vanderbilt University Medical Center's Center for Patient and Professional Advocacy, says, "One of the best ways we honor people who do the right thing is to address those who don't." Dr. Hickson notes that it's all about the expectations you have for yourself and your coworkers when someone "stubs a toe." Do you expect that all employees will be held accountable when they haven't lived out the organization's standards and values? Do you expect that others will be open to feedback? If some people are allowed to miss the mark with no opportunity to learn how their behavior appears to others, the organization has failed to live up to your expectations. Your morale—and possibly your own behavior—will suffer.

I really like the "stub a toe" phrase. We all realize that anyone can stub a toe from time to time. Even our best performers will sometimes stub a toe, quite unintentionally. And, as I'm sure you've guessed, that's where this conversational model gets its name. (A special thank-you is due to Donna Gray, chief nursing officer at St. Mary Mercy Medical Center in Livonia, MI, who began calling this model the Stub Your Toe Conversation when using it with her team.)

In short, Stub Your Toe Conversations give you a structure to remind offenders that their behavior was perceived to be inappropriate or not professional so that they will (hopefully!) not repeat it.

Vanderbilt Lowers Malpractice Lawsuit Risks with Tiered Conversations

The Stub Your Toe Conversation tough conversation model is based on research, experience, and curriculum developed by the Center for Patient and Professional Advocacy at Vanderbilt University in Nashville. As an integrated delivery system, Vanderbilt and many of its partner organizations have the ability to track patient-reported concerns about their healthcare experience. Vanderbilt also analyzes how those complaints impact inpatient and outpatient risk exposure. The researchers found that physicians at higher risk for lawsuits had a pattern of multiple concerns reported by patients over an extended period of time.

To help lower malpractice lawsuit risk, the Center designed a tiered model for addressing professionals whose patients have reported complaints about their healthcare experience. As part of the Vanderbilt onboarding orientation, all providers learn about this model so that they can address disrespectful or unsafe behaviors from any member of the team. This program, along with other safety, quality, and risk prevention efforts, has enabled the organization to dramatically reduce malpractice claims.

In Vanderbilt's tiered model, the first step in addressing undesirable behavior is a respectful and collegial (non-hierarchical, non-punitive, non-directive) "Cup of Coffee" Conversation in which the trained peer brings the concern to the attention of the physician or other professional whose behavior was perceived to be disrespectful or unsafe. The key to the Vanderbilt-defined Cup of Coffee Conversation is that the person initiating the conversation has seen or heard the concerning behavior, *or*, through organizational process and institutional policy, has the responsibility to review and (as appropriate) follow up on reports of undesirable behavior made by others.

At Studer Group we have narrowed the focus of Stub Your Toe Conversations so they do not include discussions about third-party-reported occurrences. This modification enables organizations to more easily cascade Stub Your Toe training to all staff members. However, it is still incumbent upon organizations to have policies and training in place that enable leaders to respond to complaints about disruptive professionals and other healthcare team members.

Organizations interested in additional information about Vanderbilt's Cup of Coffee research and training should review these resources:

Hickson GB, Pichert JW, Webb LE, Gabbe SG. A complementary approach to promoting professionalism: identifying, measuring, and addressing unprofessional behaviors, Acad Med. 2007; 82(11):1040-1048.

Reiter CE, Hickson GB, Pichert JW. Addressing behavior and performance issues that threaten quality and patient safety: What your attorneys want you to know. Prog Pediatr Cardio. 2012; 33(1), January: 37–45.

http://www.mc.vanderbilt.edu/root/vumc.php?site=cppa&doc=45627

http://www.mc.vanderbilt.edu/root/vumc.php?site=cppa&doc=45819

When Should I Have a Stub Your Toe Conversation?

A Stub Your Toe Conversation is appropriate when the person initiating the conversation has *seen or heard* the offending behavior. This is critical. If a third party initiates the Stub

Your Toe Conversation, you may enter into the dreaded "triangulated conversation" in which Person C tries to resolve an issue that could have been (and usually, should have been) resolved between Person A and Person B. Triangulated conversations typically result in denials and finger pointing, with Person C trying to determine the accuracy of Person A's and Person B's conflicting accusations. (We'll discuss triangulated conversations in Chapter 12.)

This point is so important, I will repeat it. In order for a Stub Your Toe Conversation to be effective, the person initiating the conversation must have *seen or heard* the offending behavior.

First, let's look at what constitutes an "offending behavior." Generally, offending behaviors are words or actions that violate any type of rule that is commonly known and a requirement of employment in the organization; for example, a behavior that is contrary to your organizational Standards of Behavior, values, or policies. (Standards of Behavior are a great tool to help inform an organization's employees about what is appropriate and what isn't—see Chapter 8 for best practices.)

Here are some examples of behaviors that might prompt a Stub Your Toe Conversation:

- Abrupt or disrespectful behavior or language.

- Passive or passive-aggressive actions or language.

- Complaining and/or gossiping. These are never okay, but their adverse impact is compounded when the behavior is witnessed by patients or family members.

- Talking "about" rather than "to" each other; i.e., the dreaded triangulated conversation.

- Incongruent words and actions. For example, your organization has a 5/10 rule that all employees have agreed to observe. (The 5/10 rule dictates that you make eye contact when someone is within 10 feet of you and greet them when they are within 5 feet of you.) You observe someone walk right by a patient or colleague without acknowledging them.

- Failure to comply with a policy, regulation, or Standard of Behavior. For instance: not wearing a nametag; not updating whiteboards in patients' rooms; tardiness; failure to document an hourly round, refrigerator temperature check, or bathroom cleaning time for a public restroom.

An offending behavior is a bit like pornography—you'll know it when you see it.

Now, let's examine why it is important for the person who sees or hears this troublesome behavior to say something. If they don't:

- It will send the message that the actions were okay. What we permit we promote.

- It breaks down trust and impairs the team's ability to function effectively.

- Continued bad behavior can take other staff members' focus off their jobs. Instead, they will direct energy toward complaining about the team member whose behavior is not consistent with standards and policies.

- It can decrease quality and increase the risk of errors. (Alan Rosenstein, MD, has researched and documented the negative impact of disruptive behaviors that are not addressed. Staff may leave, patient care may be compromised, and patient death may even occur.[1])

- Poor customer service can result.

- Support for your organizational mission may wane.

- Job satisfaction will decrease for employees and providers who are complying with organizational standards and policies.

One final note on when to have a Stub Your Toe Conversation: It's best to use this model when the undesirable behavior you observe is a first-time occurrence. (Often, first-time offenders are caring, committed, and competent employees who have simply "stubbed their toe" and need to be reminded of appropriate behavior.) If this is *not* the first time you have observed and addressed the undesirable behavior, it's probably time to move to the next difficult conversation model: the Impact Message (which we will look at in the next chapter).

Can I Have Stub Your Toe Conversations Outside My Chain of Command?

As I coach leaders and staff on how and when to have Stub Your Toe Conversations, I ask, "If you see or hear troublesome behavior, is it your place to bring it to the other person's attention?" It's easy to answer "yes" when the offender is an employee in the leader's hierarchy; maybe even when it's a peer leader or peer employee. But workshop participants are not quite as sure when the offender is an employee in another leader's department, a boss, or a healthcare provider.

If you're unsure of whether it's your "place" to have a Stub Your Toe Conversation with someone else, remember, you have personally seen or heard behavior that is contrary to your organization's standards, values, or policies. That person's peers and supervisors may not have seen the behavior. Our patients are depending on us to have these tough Stub Your Toe Conversations. Similarly, our employees want us to have these conversations when someone violates a standard or policy so they know that everyone, no matter their place in the organizational hierarchy, is being held accountable for the same criteria.

The Stub Your Toe Conversation is simply an informal conversation during which you bring your observation/experience of troublesome behavior to the awareness of your colleague. That's all there is to it. Anyone can have the conversation with anyone. There is no hierarchy. Remember, you are bringing to a colleague's attention something that appears contrary to organizational standards, values, or policy.

How Do I Conduct a Stub Your Toe Conversation?

While Stub Your Toe Conversations are meant to be held soon after an undesirable behavior is observed, you should still take a few moments to prepare. Don't open your mouth to speak before you think about what you have just experienced and what you want to communicate. Ask yourself, *What is the desired outcome? What's the intent of having the conversation? Do I need to wait for any strong emotions to pass?* When you are ready to initiate the conversation, find a place where you and the other person will be able to talk *privately*. (Remember, it is usually best to avoid sharing a concern, coaching, or criticizing in public.)

When Are Public Stub Your Toe Conversations Appropriate?

What if someone violates a policy or standard where others (besides you) personally observe the behavior? In this case, it's probably best to say something immediately so that the other witnesses know you are not condoning the behavior. Waiting to have a Stub Your Toe Conversation privately may, in fact, send the wrong message. I wouldn't recommend having a long conversation in front of others, but I would say something like, "Sarah, this isn't the time or place to discuss this. Let's take this conversation off-line and talk at the end of the meeting."

Begin the conversation by expressing your appreciation for the other person. This will help to keep the interaction positive instead of adversarial. Then review what occurred and pause to hear your colleague's views. (This is a great time to take a sip of your coffee, tea, water, or soda, if you happen to have a beverage in hand. Drinking gives you an excuse to be quiet for a moment.) Even if you disagree with the individual, listen respectfully and give them an opportunity to reflect on what you've said.

Many people will express appreciation for bringing the undesirable behavior to their attention. However, if they deny or justify the behavior, be patient and kindly suggest that while they may be correct, they should take some time to reflect on why their actions or words seemed unprofessional to you or others. Promote self-awareness or a "look in the mirror." You're not telling the person they are "bad"; you are merely relating an observation. End the conversation by once again validating the value of the person's contribution to the organization.

Here is what a Stub Your Toe Conversation might sound like:

- "Lynne, I value you as a colleague. I appreciate your experience in the organization and your ability to educate our patients in ways that make sense to them and encourage them to comply with your teaching."

- "I wanted to let you know that I just overheard the comments you made to that uninsured patient in the ED. The tone of your voice seemed less respectful than the caring professional I know you to be." Note that I didn't say "but" between the first appreciative comment and the observation comment. "But" automatically sets up a barrier and puts the receiver on the defensive.

- This is where you pause and sip or just zip your lip. More on the reaction you can anticipate in a minute.

- "I care about you and wanted to share that what I heard just now did not appear consistent with our core values."

Here are a few of the reactions you might get during the "pause" portion of this conversation:

- They might express frustration: "I am so tired of uninsured patients taking advantage of our services." "I'm frustrated that patients are using the ED instead of a doctor's office." "We are so busy and that just backs up the ED for everyone."

- They might deny that they said or did what you claim. That's why it's so important to have this conversation as quickly as possible—but again, wait until the emotion has passed.

- They might rationalize and try to place the blame on someone else. For instance, "I wasn't talking down to the patient; I was just frustrated because I was due to take my break and Suzy wasn't back yet." Here's how you might respond: "I appreciate your frustration, but we're talking about your actions. That's what I felt was inappropriate. Just because you are frustrated with Suzy isn't an excuse to take it out on one of our patients."

- They may strive for control, look out the window, or blame someone else instead of looking in the mirror and seeing their own action. "Everybody treats uninsured patients that way and you never say anything to others. What are you going to do about them?" In this situation, remember that your goal is simply to let your colleague know the behavior was observed, was concerning, and merits reflection. "I appreciate your frustration with our colleagues, but we all have to respond professionally, not take it out on one of our patients. I thought you would want to know how it appeared. Thank you for your time."

As I've said, though, the most common reaction will be one of appreciation for bringing the behavior to their attention. They'll probably be professional and remorseful. Just remember, whatever the reaction, it's about them and *not* about you.

Here are some final pointers to make the Stub Your Toe Conversation as effective as possible:

- Avoid the tendency to "fix" the problem that caused the other person to act or speak inappropriately. In other words, focus on the behavior, not its root cause. Unless there is a resource issue that you aren't aware of, your conversation should center on what you observed: the other person appearing to violate a standard, value, or policy. They are aware of the appropriate behavior, and your role is to provide a reminder about complying.

- Stay on message. This isn't the time to talk about someone else's behavior or the problems Dr. Jones is causing. You are having a Stub Your Toe Conversation to talk about a specific behavior that is inconsistent with one of your standards or values.

- Avoid the tendency to downplay or enable the behavior. If it wasn't important, why have the conversation in the first place?

- Keep it short. If the chat lasts more than four minutes, you're off track!

- Remember, it's about the action and not about the person. You are not saying the employee, provider, or volunteer is a bad person. You're telling them you saw or heard something that is uncharacteristic and unacceptable.

This is the one tough conversation model that I would highly encourage you to cascade to your entire staff. It's simple. It deals with what appear to be violations of standards, values, and policies everyone should be familiar with and everyone must adhere to. As a leader, you need to make it acceptable for anyone to have Stub Your Toe Conversations with others.

Stub Your Toe Conversation training can be done in a team meeting, but ensure you have time to do some role playing. The didactic education without role playing just isn't enough for leaders, providers, or staff. I find it most helpful to have participants create their own scenarios and then mix up the scenarios so people aren't role playing with a scenario they personally wrote. I also like to have the team keep the written scenarios, then select a new one at each team meeting or huddle and discuss how they would address the behavior.

What If I Need to Have the Same Stub Your Toe Conversation More Than Once?

What do you do if you've had a respectful Stub Your Toe Conversation with a peer, colleague, or physician and the behavior doesn't change? You spoke to John last week about wearing his nametag, and he's without it again. Or you've discussed the importance of documenting refrigerator temperature checks with Matilda, and she has once again failed to note this information on the correct chart.

When you've tried "sending the mail to the right mailbox" and the behavior persists, you need to sit down with your Human Resources rep and make sure you have a clear understanding of the disciplinary process. Stub Your Toe Conversations should be used for the high or solid/middle performer who "stubs their toe" and needs to be reminded of appropriate behavior. Someone who is consistently violating one of your organization's standards, values, or policies is truly a low performer and must be coached or disciplined appropriately.

If a Stub Your Toe Conversation after a first-time occurrence does not succeed in changing a behavior, I recommend moving to the Impact Message Conversation model (which we'll cover in the next chapter) to reinforce the consequences of the undesirable behavior.

Let's Recap:

Stub Your Toe Conversation	
Key Steps	• I value you as a colleague.
	• I saw/heard something that's inconsistent with our standards, values, or policies.
	• I wanted you to know this because I value you.

With Whom	• Colleague
	• Coworker
	• Employee
	• Another member of a committee, task force, etc.
	• Leader above you
	• Physician
	• Volunteer
	• High or middle/solid performer who "stubs their toe"
	Plus
	• Cascade to all staff so issues can be resolved at the most appropriate level
When Is This Not Appropriate	With a low performer; e.g., someone who has already been the recipient of multiple Stub Your Toe or Impact Message Conversations about performance issues. Refer to chapter on Low Performer Conversations.
Follow-up	• As appropriate if behavior doesn't change
	• Escalate to Impact Message as appropriate, *before* initiating a Low Performer Conversation

	• Escalate to Low Performer Conversation if performance doesn't change
Situations When Appropriate	• Behaviors that are or appear to be inconsistent or contrary to standards, values, or policies
	• Behavior is the exception—not a regular occurrence
Documentation	Options include:
	• In your planner or calendar
	• With an e-mail to the person
	• If the person is not someone you supervise, an e-mail to their supervisor the second time you need to speak to them

There are three things I really like about Stub Your Toe Conversations:

1. They can happen in the moment.

2. They empower the person seeing or hearing the disconcerting behavior to do something right away.

3. They are positive in nature. Anyone can "stub their toe." Stub Your Toe Conversations remind us we are all human and can make mistakes, but can recover quickly, dust ourselves off, and get back into action.

Think of Stub Your Toe Conversations as preventative medicine. When everyone on your team is empowered to recognize and address words and actions that do not align with organizational policies, values, and standards, you will be able to "diagnose" and "treat" the majority of problematic behaviors *before* they begin to infect quality of care, employee engagement, and patient satisfaction.

Chapter Four:

Impact Message

T he next tough conversation model we'll learn to use is the Impact Message. The Impact Message technique was developed and taught by my former colleague Beth Keane, to whom this book is dedicated. It's a versatile model that has applicability throughout the organization, and is ideal for a leader-to-employee conversation, a conversation between a team or committee chair and a member of the team or committee, or between colleagues. As I mentioned in the previous chapter, the Impact Message is often a logical next step to take if a Stub Your Toe Conversation does not result in the desired outcome.

There are four key steps in the Impact Message model:

1. Describe the **behavior.**

2. Describe the **impact.**

3. Indicate the desired **change.**

4. Get a **commitment.**

The core version of this model will sound like this:

1. When you…

2. The result is…

3. I need/I want/I would like…

4. Do I have your agreement?

Typically, you'll state the first three steps together, then pause to allow the other person to reflect and respond. After you've heard their input and discussed any questions or concerns, you'll end the conversation with Step 4.

While I haven't listed it in the key steps above, there's an important fifth component of a successful Impact Message: the other person's clear verbal agreement. A nod, "mmm-hmmm," "I guess," or similarly non-committal response doesn't count. You need explicit confirmation that your message was heard, understood, and will be acted on. That's why every Impact Message ends with a question to which the other person must respond.

Pretty simple, right? The "how-to" of the Impact Message is straightforward and doesn't require much explanation. It's a flexible fill-in-the-blank formula that can be applied to numerous types of difficult conversations. Throughout this chapter, I'll use examples to show you how to use the Impact Message in various types of tough conversations you may encounter.

Scenario 1: A peer, colleague, or team member consistently interrupts you. The interruption might happen while you're trying to make a point in a meeting, team huddle, or even in a one-on-one conversation.

1. "Lynne, *when you* interrupt me while I'm talking…"

2. "*The result is* that I don't feel as if I've been able to explain myself adequately."

3. "*I need you* to let me finish before you respond."

4. "*Do you agree* that you can do that?"

Scenario 2: A member of a committee you chair is consistently late to meetings.

1. "John, *when you* are consistently late to meetings…"

2. "*The result is* I feel you don't value my time or the time of others on the team."

3. "*I need* for you to be on time or let the team know you can't participate. I will no longer make others wait and recap what you've missed in the meeting if you are late, but I will make a commitment to catch you up after the meeting."

4. "*Do you agree* that you will try your best to be on time for future meetings and let us know if you are going to be late?"

Scenario 3: A team member's actions are preventing a goal from being reached. In this scenario, you can add a specific reference to the goal, as illustrated by Step 3:

1. "Suzy, *when you* open a supply pack in the OR and then don't use it…"

2. "*The result is* that the supply pack must be discarded because it has been contaminated."

3. *"Because we all share responsibility for controlling expenses…"*

4. *"I need* for you to think through the need for specific supplies and whether they are likely to be used before you open up a supply pack. It may not seem like a significant expense, but multiplied by every OR, every day, there's a lot of waste going on. Do you understand how your actions can impact the overall financial success of the surgery center?"

5. *"Do you agree* that you will be more conscientious about the use of supplies in the future? If you have questions about the use of supplies in the future, please come to me so we can discuss these implications. Okay?"

Scenario 4: The outpatient clinic or ancillary services department is not complying with a policy. Step 3 shows how you can explain why the policy is in place and why compliance is important.

By the Way, About the A-Word…

Incidentally, let's change the lexicon and call departments like radiology, lab, pharmacy, etc. *essential* services. In *Leadership for Great Customer Service*, Thom Mayer writes, "What do we call departments like radiology and laboratory services? Almost universally, you will get

> this answer: ancillary services. The term *ancillary*, though, derives from the Latin word *ankilla*, which means 'female slave.' So let's call them what they are: *essential services.*[1] When we change our wording, we may actually shift our own perception of the *impact* these professionals truly have—and thus the need for Impact Messages.

1. "*When you* don't update patients or family members in the waiting room about a delay..."

2. "*The result is* that they become anxious and worry about being late for their next appointment (or getting back to work or picking up the kids)."

3. "*We all know* that an increase in patient anxiety decreases their compliance with the prescribed treatment regime. We also know that being kept informed about waiting times is a key factor in patient satisfaction, and we are all concerned about the impact today's patient satisfaction has on word-of-mouth referrals."

4. "As we have agreed, *I need for you* to update patients every 15 minutes or sooner if you know the expected wait time has changed."

5. "*Do I have your agreement* that you will do this in the future?"

Scenario 5: You disagree with your boss and need to have a respectful conversation. This scenario would also work if you needed your boss to reconsider a new assignment.

1. *"Ms. Boss, when you* give me a new assignment and don't provide an opportunity for me to discuss options for successfully completing the project with you…"

2. *"The result is* that I get frustrated. I don't know if I should say, 'Okay' knowing I'll never be able to complete the new assignment *and* the work necessary to achieve the goals I already have, or if I should just say, 'No.'"

3. *"In the future, can you please* give me the opportunity to suggest some alternatives for reprioritizing my workload or delegating a project to someone else on my team, or to discuss how we can take something off my plate completely? I'm not trying to get out of work because I know how important each project is to our overall success. I just want to do a quality job on each task."

4. *"Can you agree* to allow me the time to discuss options with you in the future when you need to assign me or my team an additional project?"

Scenario 6: You personally observe a behavior that violates organizational policies, values, or Standards of Behavior. Does this sound like a scenario in which a Stub Your Toe Conversation might be called for? There is often some overlap between Impact Messages and Stub Your Toe Conversations.

In my experience, the step that differentiates Impact Messages from Stub Your Toe Conversations is the second part of the conversation: *The result is…* This gives you an opportunity to not only focus on the offending behavior, but also to ensure that the other person understands the impact their actions—or failure to act—is having on you, on the team, or on customer service/patient care. You wouldn't necessarily need to go into this much detail with a high performer who has experienced a one-time "toe stub," who will immediately understand the impact of their actions, and who will be internally motivated not to repeat them.

That being the case, here are a few situations in which an Impact Message might be more effective than a Stub Your Toe Conversation:

- The behavior you're addressing is *not* a first-time offense.

- The other person is a middle/solid (but *not* a high) performer who needs external motivation and encouragement to change their behavior.

- The other person is new to the team or organization, and might need help understanding the impact of their behavior.

Now, let's look at an example of how this conversation might play out:

1. "John, *when you* don't wear your nametag with your picture facing out and above your waist as prescribed in our dress code and don't keep the whiteboard up-to-date…"

2. "*The result is* that patients don't know your name and can't compliment you when I'm doing leader rounding."

3. "*I need to have you* comply with our dress code, nametag, and whiteboard policies with every patient, every day.

As you know, identifying yourself by name and qualification is an important part of AIDET® and these Key Words reduce anxiety and increase compliance with prescribed treatment protocols. That's how our patients get better."

4. *"Do I have your commitment* to follow these policies?"

AIDET: A Quick Definition

AIDET, also called the Five Fundamentals of Service, is an evidence-based tool designed to reduce patient anxiety and improve compliance. Basically, it's a communication framework that helps employees remember to use specific Key Words at Key Times^{SM} in order to help the patient feel more engaged with and comfortable about his or her care. The acronym stands for **A**cknowledge, **I**ntroduce, **D**uration, **E**xplanation, and **T**hank You. To learn more about this Studer Group tactic, please visit www.studer-group.com/AIDET.

Scenario 7: A team member is not punctual in arriving for their shift. Here, Step 3 is added to explain how tardiness affects the entire team and prevents a goal (avoiding overtime) from being reached.

1. "Matilda, *when you* are not punctual in arriving for your shift (or coming back from lunch or break on time)…"

2. "*The result is* that your team members are inconvenienced and can't do shift report/handoffs in a timely manner."

3. "This is a real concern because it results in overtime. You know we *all have a goal* to eliminate overtime."

4. "*I need to have you* plan ahead and get ready for work earlier so you can arrive promptly. That's an expectation I have of you every day."

5. "I expect you to comply with this starting at your next shift. *Will you be able to do that for me and your team members?*"

What If an Impact Message Isn't Successful?

What if you ask, "Do I have your agreement?" and the other person responds, "No, I can't do that"? Don't walk away in a huff—though you may be tempted to. Pause and take a deep breath until the emotion passes. Then continue the conversation and see if there is something short of your initial suggestion that the other person can agree to and that will resolve the problem or concern.

Let's use an example that is all too real in today's workplaces. On a periodic basis, you need to receive information from a colleague in order to complete projects. Your colleague just isn't responsive, and that has a negative impact on your ability to complete assignments on time. You have a respectful Impact Message Conversation with the colleague but their response is, "No, I can't respond within 48 hours as per our standard. I just get too much e-mail."

First, try to work with your colleague to find an alternate solution. Ask if there is someone else with whom you can work to get critical information or if there is a method you can both agree on to highlight deadlines and priorities within the subject line of your e-mails. If your colleague is still unable or unwilling to help you find a solution, you will need to approach your leader or the colleague's leader and ask for help in resolving the situation.

It's also likely that at some point you'll conduct a respectful Impact Message Conversation with a peer or colleague...but afterward, that person's behavior won't change. When you've tried "sending the mail to the right mailbox" and it sits there or is marked "return to sender," it's appropriate to escalate the concern to your leader. Be sure your leader understands that you've talked to the individual directly and the behavior has continued, even though there was an agreement that a change would take place. Sometimes this escalation is necessary, but going to a leader should never be your first step. That's when you get into triangulated conversations (see Chapter 12) where no one is the winner.

Let's Recap:

Impact Message	
Key Steps	• When you… • The result is… • I need/I want… • Do I have your agreement?
With Whom	• Colleague • Coworker • Employee • Another member of a committee, task force, etc. • Leader above you • Physician • Volunteer
When Is This Not Appropriate	With a low performer of whom you are aware; e.g., someone in your department and/or someone you supervise. Refer to chapter on Low Performer Conversations.

Follow-up	As appropriate if agreement isn't kept
Situations When Appropriate	• Persistent, repeating behavior that is disruptive to team performance, functioning of teams or committees • Peer or someone above you in organization who is exhibiting behavior inconsistent with leadership standards
Documentation	• In your planner • With an e-mail—perhaps as a thank you: *Thank you for your time today. I appreciate your understanding of the need for punctuality, compliance with the policy, etc., and your agreement to abide by the policy in the future.*

I like Impact Messages because they allow you to focus on the *why*. Explaining *why*, not just *what*, is always powerful because it enables people to understand the impact their actions and words have on outcomes, the organization, the patient experience, etc. And when people understand *why* they're being asked to do (or not to do) something, they're far more likely to comply. Used wisely, Impact Messages can be a powerful tool to help you shift employees' behaviors.

Chapter Five:

Low Performer Conversations

As leaders, we know we need to support our teams, recognize strong performance, and coach those who are trying but are still learning. But doesn't it seem that we spend an inordinate amount of time chasing after those employees who just don't care, are habitual scofflaws, and complain about everything? We'd all have more time to recognize and coach our high and middle performers if we could just get those low performers back in line.

Earlier in this book, I wrote that I don't think employees get up in the morning and say, "I'm going to work today at XYZ Health and do a crummy job"—and I stand by that assertion. If an employee isn't living up to your expectations, your first step needs to be looking in the mirror. You need to make sure you've communicated your expectations clearly and that you've provided the education and coaching the employee needs to be successful. If you can't honestly say that this is the case, a Stub Your Toe Conversation or Impact Message is usually the best place to start.

However, every leader will eventually be faced with an employee whose behavior continues to negatively impact the team's performance despite clear expectations, training, and education. When this happens, you are dealing with a low performer—and it's time to take the next step. The goal of formally addressing the low performer's behavior is (ideally) to help them become a fully contributing member of your team. Only in extreme cases do you initiate this conversation with the ultimate goal of firing the person.

As you probably already know, Low Performer Conversations can be instigated *only* by leaders. (This makes them inherently different from the other two types covered in this book.) And the Low Performer Conversation is one of the most important conversation models to have in your toolkit. For the sake of morale, employee retention, patient satisfaction, operating costs, and more, it's crucial to address low performer behavior quickly and effectively. Consider the following quotes:

- As one nursing director on a busy clinical unit in an academic medical center told Studer Group®, "I don't really mind taking care of the patients; they're the reason I went into nursing and management in the first place. It's taking care of the B-team members that wears me out. I don't know how much longer I can do it."

- Consulting colleagues from The Camden Group note, "Operating costs will need to be reduced by up to 10-20 percent over the next 3-5 years. You can't have process redesign if you haven't dealt with low performers."

If you do not move low performers up or out of your organization, they will keep the entire organization from reaching its goals of excellence.

Distinguishing Between High, Middle, and Low Performers

First, let's take a look at what, exactly, makes someone a high, middle, or low performer.

The following definitions of high, middle/solid, and low will be helpful to you, especially as you are trying to differentiate between someone who is middle/solid or low.

As you look at Figures 5.1, 5.2, and 5.3, remember that few employees have *only* low performer characteristics. Most low performers will also have some solid/middle or even high performer characteristics. However, these individuals spend most of their time in the low performer category and don't seem persuaded to change their performance, even after multiple conversations.

| FIGURE 5.1 | DEFINITION OF HIGH PERFORMER |

- **Proactive**
- **Trusted**
- **Brings solutions**
- **Teaches/precepts**
- Good attitude
- Problem solver
- You relax when you know they are on an important process improvement team
- Good influence
- Use for peer interview
- Five Pillar ownership
- Role models Standards of Behavior
- Manages up . . . not down
- Loyal to customers/patients and the organization
- Makes tough decisions
- Does not make excuses
- Knowing what you know today, would you hire this person again? ABSOLUTELY!!!

FIGURE 5.2	DEFINITION OF MIDDLE/SOLID PERFORMER
· Responsive	· Role models Standards of Behavior
· Tells you about a problem	· Manages up . . . not down
· Solid performer	· Loyal to customers/patients and the organization
· A few developmental needs	· Requires coaching to make tough decisions
· Good attendance	· Makes excuses occasionally
· Loyal most of time	· Knowing what you know today, would you hire this person again? YEAH, AND!!!
· Influenced by high and low performer	
· Wants to do a good job	
· Could just need more experience	

FIGURE 5.3	DEFINITION OF LOW PERFORMER
· Unaware/unwilling	· Thinks they will outlast the leader
· Blames you for a problem	· Does not role model Standards of Behavior
· Advocates for the status quo	· Manages down staff, peers, or the organization
· Even complains about free food	· Loyal to staff rather than customers/patients
· Points out problems in a negative way	· Avoids making tough decisions and taking action
· Positions leadership poorly	· Makes excuses to rationalize lack of results
· Master of "we/they"	· Knowing what you know today, would you hire this person again? NEVER!!!
· Blames higher-ups	
· Passive-aggressive	

Can Pizza Identify Low Performers?

When you got to the low performer definition, you probably chuckled about "even complains about free food." I know we can't do this (HR would send us directly to jail!), but it's tempting to order cheese pizza for everyone, see who complains that there's no pepperoni pizza, identify those folks as low performers, and invite them off the bus!

Since this chapter is devoted to the Low Performer Conversation model, let's examine this category of employee in more detail. There are several traits and behaviors that are common to low performers and that distinguish them from, say, middle performers who simply aren't receiving the education and support they need, or high performers on a "toe-stub" day. Figure 5.4 lists low performer traits and behaviors:

FIGURE 5.4	LOW PERFORMER TRAITS AND BEHAVIORS
TRAIT	**LOW PERFORMER BEHAVIORS**
Definition	Points out problems in a negative way. Positions leadership poorly. Master of we/they. Passive-aggressive. Thinks they will outlast the leader. Says manager is the problem.
Professionalism	Does not communicate effectively about absences from work areas. Handles personal phone calls in a manner that interferes with work. Breaks last longer than allowed.
Teamwork	Demonstrates little commitment to the work unit and the organization.
Knowledge & Competence	Shows little interest in improving their own performance or the performance of the organization. Develops professional skills only when asked.
Communication	Comes to work with an attitude that is manifested in negative behaviors. Has a negative influence on the work environment.
Safety Awareness	Performs work with little regard for the behaviors of safety awareness.

For more tools to help you distinguish between high, middle, and low performers and conduct conversations with each group, please visit www.studergroup.com/highmiddlelow.

An Alternate View of High, Middle, and Low Performers

Another definition of high, middle, and low performers comes from Richard Corder, assistant vice president of business development for CRICO Strategies, located in Boston. Instead of high, middle, and low performers, Richard suggests we call these employees orchids, daisies, and weeds. (I especially like this analogy because my husband is a botanist.) The definitions may surprise you.

- Orchids are the low performers. They need to be constantly managed.

- Daisies are the solid/middle performers. They need a little more care in the form of coaching.

- Weeds are the high performers. They can grow and thrive anywhere. They just need mentoring.

FIGURE 5.5 | ALTERNATE VIEW OF highmiddlelow®

The Two Types of Low Performers

As Figure 5.6 illustrates, there are actually two types of low performers: those who fall short on performance results (e.g., competencies and achieving goals) and those who do not adhere to standards (e.g., violating values or policies). Sometimes, a low performer will fall into both categories. Before initiating a tough conversation, it's critical that you know which type of low performer you are dealing with, and that you are able to support your determination with quantitative results and specific examples. (Note that high or solid/middle performers are doing an acceptable, if not outstanding, job on both of these scales.)

FIGURE 5.6 | DIFFERENTIATING THE TWO TYPES OF LOW PERFORMERS

- Has Skill
- Needs Will

HIGH

PERFORMANCE RESULTS
Measured by Manager Evaluation and Scorecard

MIDDLE

LOW

- Has Will
- Needs Skill

STANDARDS OF BEHAVIOR
Measured by Manager Evaluation and Annual Customer Evaluations

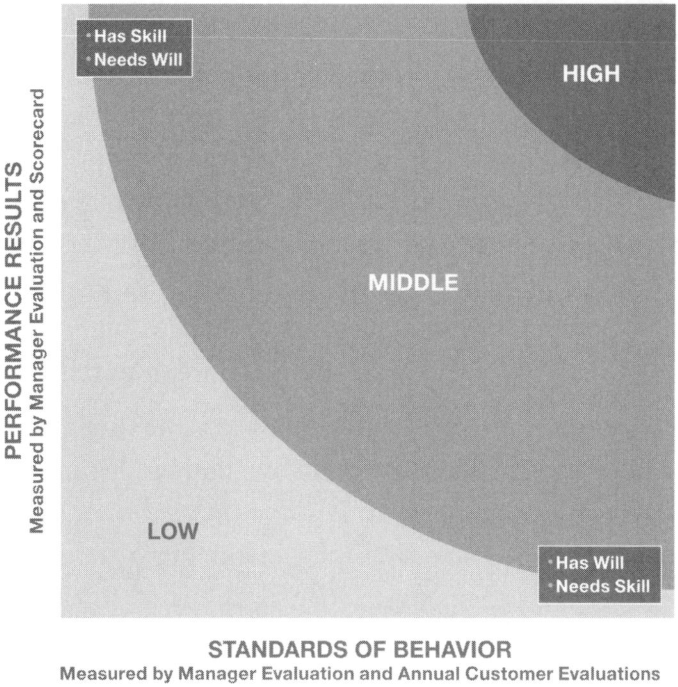

The low performer who falls in the bottom right of the graph is often practicing your Standards of Behavior and role modeling your values and is easy for you to deal with. Unfortunately, this person can't perform the tasks associated with the job. In other words, they have the will but need the skill. This type of low performer can often learn what they need to know when you invest in coaching and training—but not always. If you coach, counsel, train, and retrain this person and they still aren't performing as expected, your path forward is clear: It's time to move them off the bus. Even if the employee is really nice and loves the organization, those positive characteristics don't make up for a lack of competencies.

It's the upper left low performer who presents your biggest challenge. This is the employee or provider who has incredible clinical skills or other job competencies—they may even be your most skilled nurse or surgeon—but they consistently demonstrate behaviors that are contrary to your standards and values. In short, they have the skill but need the will. This person is actually a low performer and needs to be coached, counseled, and moved off the bus if their performance doesn't improve. It's NOT appropriate to recycle that person to another department or promote them. You must have the low performer conversation with them, put them on a performance plan, and (as Disney would say) "invite them to find their happiness elsewhere" if their performance doesn't improve.

All over the country, I hear about the same nurse who was a "high performer" (clinically, anyway), but with whom no one wanted to work because of an attitude that led to negative behaviors. Instead of counseling this person, organizations move them to Home Health. Now, I love Home Health team members as much as any other department, but the worst place for a low performer is in my grandmother's home without super-vision. Shame on us!

How Do I Conduct a Low Performer Conversation?

So, once you have identified the low performers on your team and determined the areas in which they need to improve, how do you conduct the Low Performer Conversation?

First, do your homework. Meet with your boss and your HR partner as soon as possible to ensure that you have a clear understanding of the disciplinary process. *I can't stress the importance of this step enough.* You need to assure yourself that you know what documentation is necessary to begin the formal disciplinary process and that you will be in compliance with any requirements if the employee is covered by a union or other employment contract. (The fact that an employee is in a union doesn't mean you can't terminate them. It just means it's even more important that you follow due process and the necessary grievance process steps.)

Once you are sure that you have gathered the documentation you need and understand your organization's disciplinary process, it's time to have a conversation with the low performer. We at Studer Group use the DESK model.

1. The first step is to *Describe* the behavior that has been observed.

2. Then *Evaluate* how you feel about this behavior.

3. Next, ensure the employee or provider knows what good behavior looks like. You can *Show* them the proper

procedure or assign them a mentor or buddy who will demonstrate the appropriate behavior.

4. Finally, make sure the employee *Knows* the consequences if their behavior doesn't change. Involve your HR partner from the beginning so you know what consequences are appropriate and the process that will be followed (more on this later in the chapter).

Right off the bat, the DESK model is different from Stub Your Toe Conversations and Impact Messages. This conversation does *not* begin on a positive note. Anyone who forgets this caveat is setting themselves up for trouble right away. Yes, I know that's contrary to everything your mom told you about "if you can't say something nice, don't say anything." In this instance, however, if you start out with a positive comment, that's all the low performer will remember about your conversation. You must be serious right from the beginning.

Also, keep in mind that it is easier to have a Low Performer Conversation if you have excellent Standards of Behavior (which we'll discuss in Chapter 8) that have been signed by all employees and providers upon employment or credentialing. I remember an organization that had a Home Health nurse who was a great clinician but refused to complete her paperwork. They couldn't think of any way to coach her. I reminded them that they had a Standard of Financial Stewardship, which meant that if the nurse wasn't completing her paperwork, the Home Health Agency couldn't bill for her work. She was in violation of a standard. After this was pointed out, her performance improved.

Let's look at how the Low Performer Conversation with this Home Health nurse might have gone:

1. "Suzanne, we need to have a serious conversation this morning. You are aware that a requirement of your job is to complete all required paperwork within two days of seeing a patient. Not only is this a competency described in your job description, but it's also a requirement of our Financial Stewardship Standard of Behavior."

2. "I'm disappointed in you. We've had this conversation before and your performance hasn't changed."

3. "Tomorrow, I'm going to have you work with Emily from the business office to ensure you know how to successfully complete this paperwork. Emily will report to me at the end of the day on your aptitude for learning these procedures."

4. "Going forward, I will be reviewing your work weekly, and I expect that we will talk once a week about your compliance. I expect your performance to meet these standards immediately. If there are continuing gaps, we will need to have a different conversation and move to the first step in our disciplinary process. You have a choice to make. In the future, will you adhere to policies and procedures and complete your paperwork on time? If not, we'll move to another conversation. Do you have any questions?"

Here is another example—this time about a medical assistant who isn't restocking rooms at the end of his shift. A similar conversation could occur with a lab tech/assistant who isn't leaving the work area clean, or a business office/registration/admitting clerk who doesn't process all of his/her paperwork before the end of the shift. You get the picture.

1. "Manuel, we need to have a serious conversation this afternoon. One of the tasks you are to perform each day before the end of your shift is restocking each of the exam rooms your doctors use so they are prepared and ready to go the next morning. When you don't complete this assignment as required, you place an unnecessary burden on your coworkers and often delay the rooming of the first patients the next morning. Not only is this a requirement spelled out in your job description, but it also relates to our Standards of Teamwork and Timeliness."

2. "I'm disappointed in you. We've talked about this before and your performance doesn't seem to change."

3. "As clinic lead, I've asked Kathryn to shadow you tomorrow and give you tips on how to accomplish all of your tasks within your scheduled shift. Please accept her coaching in the professional manner of which I know you are capable."

4. "I will be checking your rooms at the end of each day for the next week and will give you feedback on your progress in achieving this competency. We will formally meet again at this time next week. If your performance hasn't improved, it will be necessary for me to write you up and begin a more formal disciplinary process. Do you have any questions?"

A final word of advice: Don't go into a Low Performer Conversation "cold." Know exactly what you want to say. Prepare and practice. Then practice some more. You never know how the low performer is going to respond. They have a whole bag of tricks they can draw upon once they comprehend the seriousness of the situation. (These "tricks" might include rolling their eyes, tapping their fingers, shifting the conversation's focus to others, etc.) The more clear the desired outcome is in your mind, the greater your chance of (finally!) motivating a low performer to change their behavior...or obtaining the documentation you need to move them out of the organization.

The Importance of Follow-Through

You probably noticed in both of the previous examples that the leader notified the low performer of follow-up meetings. Why is this so important?

It's likely that this employee has been a low performer since kindergarten. Parents, teachers, coaches, and other employers have all had Low Performer Conversations with this person to no avail. Why not? Because there was no follow-through. After all, it's hard work to move, coach, and counsel a low performer, and even harder to move them off the bus. The process is unpleasant and time consuming, so most people avoid it.

Without committed follow-through, your Low Performer Conversation will have little to no impact. As a result, employee dissatisfaction, provider dissatisfaction, and patient dissatisfaction will persist. Our employees, providers, and patients deserve better than having to work with or be cared for by a low performer.

Studer Group recommends following up with low performers on a very regular basis after having a conversation with them. I have found that weekly conversations with low performers work well. Be sure to discuss their compliance and the progress of their performance improvement plan. Finally, document each meeting. If performance does *not* improve, you will most likely need this documentation to move the person out of the organization.

Remember, while they may be unpleasant to conduct, Low Performer Conversations ultimately have a positive impact. If performance does not improve, you allow the low performer to move on to an organization that will be a better fit for them. And whether the low performer moves on *or* improves their current performance, you free yourself up to develop and nurture the middle and high performers who will be the future of the organization.

Let's Recap:

Low Performer Conversation

Key Steps	• **D**: Describe
	Describe what has been observed.
	• **E**: Evaluate
	Evaluate how you feel.

- **S**: Show

  Show what needs to be done.

- **K**: Know

  Know the consequences of continued same performance.

With Whom	Employees you supervise who fit the definition of low performer
When Is This Not Appropriate	• If proper documentation has not been completed • If HR and your immediate supervisor have not been involved (to ensure the correct procedure is being followed)
Follow-up	• Action plan with weekly meetings until behavior/performance conforms • Move to advanced forms of discipline as appropriate and in concert with your HR rep
Situations When Appropriate	• Employee demonstrates characteristics of a low performer • Pattern of behavior is persistent • Behavior is detrimental to patient or employee safety

Documentation	Consistent with your disciplinary action policy:

- Verbal warning
- Written warning
- Final warning
- Discharge

The three conversational models have been designed to give you the tools you need to constructively confront your low performers for the good of *everyone* on your team. By having Stub Your Toe Conversations as incidents occur and following up with Impact Messages when the behavior is repeated, you will build a foundation that allows Low Performer Conversations to happen when the time is right. In this way, the three models work together to keep all employees focused on the organization's values and mission. Used carefully and consistently, they will greatly improve your culture.

Part Two:

Tools to Support
Tough Conversations

CHAPTER SIX:

THE IMPORTANCE OF PRACTICE

Yes, you've read about the three models for conducting difficult conversations—but that alone won't enable you to flawlessly execute the next tough conversation you need to have with a colleague, employee, physician, or boss. Your own nervousness and discomfort, or unexpected pushback from the other person, are just two of the many possibilities that could cause everything you've learned to fly right out of your head at a critical moment! That's why practice is so important.

Use Team Meetings to Practice Tough Conversations

Team meetings and leadership training sessions—often called Leadership Development Institutes (LDI) by those who work with Studer Group®—provide excellent opportunities to teach leaders and staff about the three conversational models and to allow employees to build their skills through practice. (A brief aside: Remember that you won't teach every employee about every conversational model. For instance, only leaders would be in a position to have a Low Performer Conversation with someone else. As I mentioned in Chapter 3, however, I do recommend that you cascade the Stub Your Toe Conversation model to all of your staff members.)

When teaching teams how to have tough conversations, I always ask participants to practice using role-play. I used to spend hours brainstorming and writing the best scenarios I could think of. Then I got smart and realized that an organization or department's own leaders (or team members) could write much more realistic scenarios than I could! Now I hand out 3 x 5 cards at every training session and ask each participant to write a brief scenario setting up a tough conversation they know they need to have.

I recommend that you adopt this strategy, too. Ask that team members *not* identify the conversation as Stub Your Toe, Impact Message, or Low Performer. They should simply describe the behavior that needs to be addressed, as well as its impact. Once the scenarios have been written, divide your team into groups of three (triads), mix up the cards, and distribute them equally to each group.

Now, instruct each team to role-play the scenarios it has been given. For each scenario, one person will play the role of the leader, another will play the employee with whom the leader is having the conversation, and the third person will serve as an observer who provides feedback. Make sure each person has an opportunity to play each role. Remind observers that they should provide positive feedback *before* offering coaching suggestions to their teammates. (Remember, people are much more receptive to constructive criticism when they have first been reminded of the things they have done well.)

Once you've done the initial tough conversation training, hold on to your scenario cards! At each subsequent team meeting or huddle, you can select a card from the pile and discuss as a group how you'd approach the conversation. This will keep everyone on their toes and keep the learning fresh.

As time goes by, continue to add to your scenario library based on what's happening in your organization. Your list of scenarios should be a living, breathing compendium of possible situations that we all will encounter in our careers.

Schedule Some Personal Practice

So, what can you do if you need to have a tough conversation and you don't have a tough conversation training or team meeting coming up? Grab another leader, colleague, or friend and describe the scenario you are facing. Give them some tips on how to role-play the offending employee or coworker. Then practice the conversation. Together, evaluate how the interaction went, hit replay, and try again. You'll both be better for having this experience.

Scenarios for Practice

The remainder of this chapter contains over a dozen difficult conversation scenarios written by healthcare leaders. Although I compiled more than 100 potential scenarios while writing this book, I've selected the ones I most commonly encounter all over the country. For each scenario, I've given you some key words to use as a conversation starter.

As you read through this list, see if you agree with the type of conversational model I would use for each scenario and the key words I'd include in the conversation. There are always opportunities for improvement!

SCENARIO 1

Scenario

A staff member is technically strong and has a lot of tenure but is resistant to change. She has been heard speaking negatively about her new manager and initiatives the manager is putting in place.

Type of Tough Conversation in Response

Start with a Stub Your Toe Conversation or Impact Message. Escalate to Low Performer if the behavior doesn't change.

Key Words

"Sarah, I value your skills and technical expertise. I appreciate having you on the team. When you speak negatively about Sam and the new concepts he's bringing to the department to help us operate more efficiently, you put a negative cloak over all of us. I think Sam is on the right track. I think you should give his ideas a chance and see if they can help us. I don't want to hear any more of your complaints."

SCENARIO 2

Scenario

A staff member is observed speaking negatively about the Emergency Department to another staff member in front of a patient brought to the unit.

Type of Tough Conversation in Response

Stub Your Toe Conversation

Key Words

"George, I value your expertise in treating and caring for our critically ill patients. Remember, it's never appropriate to speak negatively in front of patients and family members. If you have problems with the ED, you should talk to our supervisor. Or you can bring your concerns up in a team meeting so we can give our supervisor examples she can use in a meeting with the ED director. It's inappropriate to express your concerns to other staff members, especially when a patient is there."

SCENARIO 3

Scenario

The department volume is down, and the spending is over budget. This has been going on for two months.

Type of Tough Conversation in Response

Impact Message

Key Words

At a team meeting: "We have a challenge facing us. Our volumes are down but our spending on supplies hasn't decreased. This can't continue. We have to make a change. I'd like to do some brainstorming on how we can get our spending in line until volumes return to projected levels. Can I have your participation and support?"

SCENARIO 4

Scenario

A secretary is overheard talking about how she went into her brother-in-law's chart and looked at his lab work.

Type of Tough Conversation in Response

Start with a Stub Your Toe Conversation and move quickly to "off the bus" if appropriate.

Key Words

First, clarify what happened. If it's truly a HIPAA violation, suspension or dismissal is appropriate. "Sarah, I think I'm hearing you say something that is uncharacteristic and is a potential violation of our standards and policies. Are you saying that you went into a patient's chart, without permission, just for your personal information? If so, that's a HIPAA violation that could lead to your suspension or dismissal. Tell me what you were doing."

SCENARIO 5

Scenario

A part-time employee was hired to work 15-22 hours a week. Her father was placed in comfort care, and she was provided time off. She has returned to work and has told her supervisor she can work only 15 hours a week—no more—and only on certain days.

Type of Tough Conversation in Response

First, check with your HR partner about options. Is the employee eligible for FMLA? Does the employee need to take additional time off, etc.?

Key Words

Base conversations on what you hear from HR. Maybe a Stub Your Toe Conversation would be appropriate. "Christine, I was so sorry to hear about your father. I know this has been a really hard time for you. However, the job you do is designed to serve a need—to provide the very best care for our patients. Often, that care requires that a caregiver be here longer than 15 hours a week and it may not be limited to certain days. Are you certain you cannot meet these expectations?" (You might segue into the HR options here.)

SCENARIO 6

Scenario

A long-time employee is observed behaving in a disrespectful manner to other team members by his peers. He is also noted to be rude to providers and families on the phone. The most recent incident included the employee's unwillingness to cover his teammate for dinner. As a result, the teammate didn't get dinner until late in shift.

Type of Tough Conversation in Response

Consider a Stub Your Toe Conversation or Impact Message unless you've already talked to this employee and he is exhibiting Low Performer behavior.

Key Words

"Wayne, what's going on? Usually you are a productive team player, but in recent days I've observed you being rude to peers, providers, and families. That's not like you. Is something wrong that you'd like to talk about? This behavior cannot persist at work. Maybe you need to take some time off or make an appointment with Employee Assistance to talk through the problem."

SCENARIO 7

Scenario

A patient complains about the doctor's attitude—he's not listening to the patient. You have raised this issue with the doctor before.

Type of Tough Conversation in Response

Stub Your Toe Conversation

Key Words

"Dr. Jones, I'm concerned. Clinically, I think you are a very good provider. We've talked in the past about concerns patients have that you don't listen to them. I've heard additional complaints from my patients yesterday and today. Is there something I can do to help the patients perceive that you are skilled and do want to listen? Listening and being heard is one of the key behaviors that will reduce the patients' anxiety, improve their compliance, and speed their recovery. I'm happy to help you. How will you ensure that this behavior doesn't continue?"

SCENARIO 8

Scenario

An employee has many personal demands at home; e.g., an ill spouse or child. Despite coaching and specific direction, the employee is not making the necessary and expected changes in procedures.

Type of Tough Conversation in Response

Impact Message, moving to Low Performer

Key Words

"Julia, I know this is a stressful time for you at home. When you consistently refuse to make the expected changes in our procedures, the result is that you are negatively impacting the performance of the entire team. Is there something you don't understand about the new expectations that I need to go over again? Would it be helpful for you to take some time off right now and come back when you can focus 100% on the job when you are here? I need your commitment to these new procedures if you want to continue working in the department."

SCENARIO 9

Scenario

A coworker expresses strong opinions in team meetings that often offend other team members.

Type of Tough Conversation in Response

Impact Message

Key Words

"John, I know you have lots of good ideas and strong opinions. When you express your opinions in team meetings using that harsh tone, you are offending others. Then they are discouraged from speaking up, too. I need for you to temper your opinions and wait for others to speak first. Do I have your commitment to make this change?"

SCENARIO 10

Scenario

A staff member is using Facebook on her cell phone in a patient care area where other staff members and patients witness the event.

Type of Tough Conversation in Response

Stub Your Toe Conversation

Key Words

"Sally, you're a great coworker and I like working with you. I feel very uncomfortable when it's obvious you are using your cell phone to access Facebook in patient care areas. You know that's against our policies. You can use your cell on breaks. Let's focus on patients when we're with them."

SCENARIO 11

Scenario

A manager addresses individual staff issues in front of a large group or in a loud voice.

Type of Tough Conversation in Response

Impact Message

Key Words

"Tony, I know I needed that coaching. When you make that type of comment using a loud voice and in front of others, the result is that I get defensive and angry. I'm happy to be coached. I want to get better. I just need to have you provide this type of feedback privately so we can discuss next steps in a professional manner. Would you please do that in the future?"

SCENARIO 12

Scenario

A team member is not providing accurate and honest project status updates.

Type of Tough Conversation in Response

Impact Message

Key Words

"Antoinette, I know that you want to always portray the team in the most positive light. Others are counting on us to provide reports that are timely and accurate so that they can complete their own tasks in the chain of events. When you provide an unrealistic and inaccurate project status update, the result is that others can't depend on us to support the team. Since we all want the organization to succeed, we need to always be honest, timely, and accurate with our project updates. Can you please do that in the future?"

SCENARIO 13

Scenario

A physician shouts at a nurse for not carrying out orders correctly.

Type of Tough Conversation in Response

Stub Your Toe Conversation

Key Words

"Dr. Smith, I respect your clinical skills and want to learn from you. When you are unhappy with the way I have done something, I want you to tell me about it. That can best be done in a private setting away from other staff and patients and in a calm voice. It is never appropriate to yell or demean me—or anyone else—and I feel that's what you just did."

SCENARIO 14

Scenario

An employee has body odor.

Type of Tough Conversation in Response

Stub Your Toe Conversation

Key Words

"Sandra, I need to have a tough conversation with you. Patients and staff have talked to me about you having unpleasant body odor, and this is something I've personally noticed as well. Do you know what is causing this? (pause) Perhaps you need to talk to a physician to see if there is something medically behind this problem."

SCENARIO 15

Scenario

A receptionist answers the phone in a flat voice and sounds abrupt, as though she doesn't have time to listen to the caller. She gives the impression that she's in a hurry and being interrupted.

Type of Tough Conversation in Response

Impact Message

Key Words

"Sharon, when you answer the phone using a rushed or abrupt voice and flat tone, the result is that our patients feel you are not pleased to have them call. Because we are here to serve our patients, I need you to use a pleasing tone and cheerful voice when answering the phone. Will you please do that in the future? If you need to practice with someone, I'd be happy to call you periodically and give you feedback on how you are doing."

SCENARIO 16

Scenario

A staff member's clothing is too revealing. Her name badge is on a long lanyard rather than worn at eye level.

Type of Tough Conversation in Response

Stub Your Toe Conversation

Key Words

"Sarah, you are doing an excellent job registering patients in a timely manner. You really have learned the many steps in this administrative process very quickly. I do want you to remember that we have a departmental dress code. It prescribes that everyone will wear modest clothing and that nametags will be worn so they can easily be seen at eye level. I expect everyone to abide by the dress code and you're out of compliance right now. Today, I'd like you to go to the break room and wear one of the extra sweaters there over your blouse. Also, please move your nametag up to your collar. With these changes, not only will your work performance be excellent but you'll also have the professional appearance expected in this department."

SCENARIO 17

Scenario

A nurse consistently tells patients that someone else will help them.

Type of Tough Conversation in Response

Impact Message

Key Words

"Tom, when you tell your patients that someone else will be in to help them and then don't follow through, the result is that your patients' needs are not being served and they are losing confidence in you. I need to have you address your patients' needs when you are with them during your Hourly Rounding® visits. If that isn't possible, immediately ask another team member to help and then follow through on your next visit. Can I count on you to start doing that with the next patient request you receive?"

SCENARIO 18

Scenario

An employee is immediately transferring calls to the clinic instead of listening and addressing the patient's scheduling needs.

Type of Tough Conversation in Response

Impact Message

Key Words

"Tony, I need for you to listen to the patients' requests before you transfer them to the appointment desk. When you don't listen to the patients' complete request, you are likely to transfer them to the wrong party. That's frustrating to our patients and they will get the impression we don't care. Do you need some additional orientation and training to be able to accommodate patients' requests when they call? If not, in the future, I'll expect you to listen carefully to the patients' full requests before transferring them."

SCENARIO 19

Scenario

An employee speaks negatively about her peers to others.

Type of Tough Conversation in Response

Stub Your Toe Conversation

Key Words

"Irene, when I was coming into the break room just now, I overhead you speaking negatively about some of your coworkers on another shift. That's not living our value of Teamwork. If you have concerns about someone else's performance in the future, I expect you to use the Stub Your Toe skills you have been taught to speak with them directly, or come to me with specific examples of your concerns. You're a good CNA and spreading gossip just isn't consistent with our performance standards."

When you are selected to be a leader in your department, the ability to successfully conduct difficult conversations isn't magically conferred on you. These are learned skills, and they need to be continually practiced and nurtured. And trust me—just when you think you've become very good at one type of tough conversation, another scenario will appear that will require you to dust off what you've learned and practice some more.

Mastering tough conversations isn't something you do only once, but a skill that you need to build throughout your career and throughout your life (or as long as you'll be interacting with other human beings!).

CHAPTER SEVEN:

CONSEQUENCES, RECOGNITION, AND REWARDS

For difficult conversations to be considered "successful," the other person must change their behavior based on what was discussed. But as all leaders know, long-term compliance doesn't always happen on its own. It is often supported by two important tools: rewards and consequences.

When an employee's performance improves, a reward will encourage them to repeat the behavior. Everyone appreciates positive recognition for a job well done! On the other hand, if the employee's performance does not improve, consequences will make it clear that compliance is expected and important. (And if the employee's behavior still does not change, consequences like formal disciplinary procedures allow you to move that person off the bus.)

In this chapter, we will examine the importance of both consequences and rewards, and how to apply them in a way that drives positive change after tough conversations.

Consequences Must Be Mandatory

First, let's look at consequences.

Studer Group's® Bob Murphy has done some interesting research at our institutes and conferences. He has asked leaders what words are best to set performance expectations and drive compliance. Here are the results:

- If the senior leader says a behavior is "expected," only about 26 percent of leaders feel they must comply.

- If the senior leader elevates the word to "required," a full 69 percent of leaders feel they must comply.

- It isn't until the senior leader uses the word "mandatory" that almost all leaders—a full 98 percent—feel they must comply.

(FYI, these percentages are based on live audience polling. The data represents the responses of more than 10,000 people who responded "must" when asked the question, "When you hear the word _____, do you think "must" or "should"?")

FIGURE 7.1 | WORDS THAT DRIVE COMPLIANCE IN HOSPITALS

26% EXPECTED   69% REQUIRED   98% MANDATORY

Clearly, the words we use matter—and not just between senior leaders and their direct reports. Keep Figure 7.1 in mind during difficult conversations with all employees. Avoid using "expected," "required," and "mandatory" as interchangeable synonyms, because listeners will respond differently to each.

If you want a behavior to change, use the word "mandatory"—but only if you are ready and willing to enforce consequences for noncompliance. Often, the other person will be violating a policy, standard, or value, and your organization will have a formal disciplinary procedure in place for just such an occurrence. "Mandatory" will sometimes be helpful in Impact Messages and will almost always be necessary in Low Performer Conversations.

Bear in mind that if the other person doesn't comply with a "mandatory" change and there are no consequences, you've created a permit/promote situation. (As Studer Group speaker Liz Jazwiec says, "What you permit, you promote.") Without consequences for noncompliance, the other person will have no reason to change their behavior. (Remember, in

Chapter 5 I noted that most low performers have remained low performers throughout their lives because no one enforced consequences!) What's more, others who observe the noncompliance may question the effectiveness of leadership and may also start to practice the behavior in question.

Consequences need to apply across the board if there is an expectation that everyone complete the task. If you let some people off the hook, others will see that you aren't committed to equal enforcement and will be less likely to complete the task next time.

Let's look at a simple example. An employee is out of compliance with the dress code. You have a conversation with the employee and ask them to put on scrubs for the rest of their shift. You also caution them that if this infraction happens again, they will be sent home. So, if the employee comes to work in violation of the dress code again, you *must* send them home—without pay—to change clothes. If you don't follow through with the consequences, others will notice and will also be tempted to break the rules.

And what if you aren't in a position to enforce consequences? For example, you've just reminded a colleague that in your organization's culture, it is mandatory to uphold certain Standards of Behavior. However, as a peer, you don't have the authority to initiate disciplinary procedures if the other person continues to violate the standards. In this situation, be sure to share the conversation with your colleague's leader. The leader may choose to immediately follow up with your peer to make sure they understand that following the standards is mandatory. The leader will also be able to initiate a disciplinary action if noncompliance continues.

Use Reward and Recognition to Hardwire Desirable Behaviors

Now let's move from consequences to reward and recognition.

If you're familiar with Studer Group's work, you know that our founder started his professional life as a special education teacher. When Quint Studer moved from education to healthcare, he brought some key principles with him. Among them were the importance of taking small steps and repeating these steps until they are hardwired, instead of striving for giant leaps forward. Why? It's much easier to get the big things right when you get the little things right first.

As any experienced leader knows, tough conversations are often part of the hardwiring process. It is our responsibility to tell team members, volunteers, and providers what they need to improve on, and to ensure that the correct changes are made. We've already talked about how consequences fit into this process. Reward and recognition have an important place as well. (Studer Group defines reward and recognition as "any act that acknowledges a valuable contribution and great work: notes, flowers, phone calls, as well as monetary incentives.")

Sure, you can get someone to change their behavior using the *do it—or else* method. However, relying solely on consequences leads to resentment, employees doing only the bare minimum, and—eventually—burnout. If you want someone's long-term enthusiasm, engagement, and buy-in, it's wiser to encourage change using positive reinforcement.

Reward and recognition can be used during and after difficult conversations in several ways. Remember that Stub

Your Toe Conversations begin with your acknowledging your colleague's contribution to the organization. This falls under Studer Group's definition of reward and recognition and serves to get the interaction started on a positive note.

Reward and recognition is also a valuable part of following up with someone after a successful outcome. If you have a tough conversation with someone and they correct the behavior you've talked about, it's so important to say, "Thank you. I'm proud of you for approaching the situation in that way. That's exactly what we were talking about." This can—and should—be done with all three conversational models.

Let's look at the same simple example as above: An employee has come to work out of compliance with the dress code, you've had them change into scrubs, and you've talked to them about the consequences of future violations. When the employee arrives to their next shift dressed appropriately, thank them and reinforce that you appreciate their adherence to the dress code.

Are You Too Busy to Say Thank You?

In our hectic world, phrases like "thank you," "good job," or "I'm proud of you" are often lost in the shuffle. It's not that we don't feel gratitude for a job well done or notice when someone else goes above and beyond; it's just that we're so caught up in busy-ness that we don't take time to verbalize these sentiments. That's a shame. Employees often say the only time they speak to their leader is when criticism is handed out. And having met many leaders, I *know* this isn't their intent. I encourage leaders (and all employees!) to recognize others as often as possible.

Recognize as Frequently as Possible

In 1997, Tom Connellan published *Inside the Magic Kingdom*, where he referenced compliment-to-complaint ratios.[1] As Figure 7.2 shows, if you give a colleague three compliments for every one complaint, the colleague feels positive. A 2:1 ratio will leave the person feeling neutral, and a 1:1 ratio actually produces negative feelings. In other words, complaints stick with us longer and carry more weight than compliments. For this reason, it's especially important to follow up difficult conversations with compliments (as long as they are earned).

FIGURE 7.2	COMPLIMENT-TO-CRITICISM RATIO	
3 to 1	3 compliments, 1 criticism	Positive!
2 to 1	2 compliments, 1 criticism	Neutral
1 to 1	1 compliment, 1 criticism	Negative

That said, don't feel bound by the 3:1 ratio. When it comes to compliments, more is better. Research by Marcial Losada and Emily Heaphy in the March 15, 2013, *Harvard Business Review* notes that top performing teams are most productive when the compliment-to-complaint ratio is higher.[2] (See Figure 7.3.)

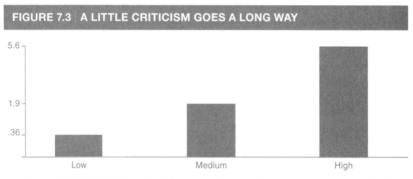

FIGURE 7.3 | A LITTLE CRITICISM GOES A LONG WAY

Source: LOSADA & HEAPHY. The role of positivity and connectivity in the performance of business teams. 2004. HER.CRG

Allow me to share one more opinion on the importance of frequent compliments: In the *Harvard Business Review* article containing the research referenced above, Jack Zenger and Joseph Folkman noted, "Only positive feedback can motivate people to continue doing what they're doing well, and do it with more vigor, determination, and creativity. The most well-intentioned criticism can rupture relationships and undermine self-confidence and initiative. It can change behavior, certainly, but it doesn't cause people to put forth their best efforts."[3]

What Types of Recognition Are Most Important to Our Team Members?

Some leaders assume that the biggest motivator of employee change is money. You might be surprised by how often this *isn't* the case! The top five workplace incentives as identified by Gerald Graham, a management professor at Wichita State University, are:

1. Written Thanks from Manager/Executive Team Leader

2. Personal Thanks from Manager

3. Promotion for Performance

4. Public Praise

5. Morale-Building Meetings[4]

It's clear that even more than financial compensation, people want to be noticed and appreciated for their efforts. They want to know they are valued members of a team, not just numbers on the payroll. (And even if they would never admit it, team members who have recently been through a difficult conversation are especially grateful for this type of reassurance.)

That said, even these "top" methods of reward and recognition are not one-size-fits-all. Some of your team members will love to be praised at a team meeting or huddle. Others would die of embarrassment in this public setting. To learn more about how your team members would like to receive reward and recognition, I recommend reading *How Full Is Your Bucket?* by Tom Rath.[5] This great little book even includes a "Bucket Filling Questionnaire" that will help you.

The Thank-You Note: An Oldie *and* a Goodie

Understandably, leaders are always on the lookout for new methods to motivate employees. (And please, do utilize fresh methods of reward and recognition as you learn about them!) But don't leave tried-and-true tactics behind.

We at Studer Group continue to find that good old-fashioned thank-you notes are appreciated by just about everyone. I say "old-fashioned" because it really matters that they are handwritten and not typed; that they are snail mailed and not emailed; that they go to the person's home and not their office inbox. You're not going to find an employee who says, "I wish my leader hadn't written a note to tell me how much she appreciates my improvement!" For this reason, the handwritten Thank-You Note is one of Studer Group's Must-Haves®.

Notes should be written to employees or providers who go "above and beyond." (This criteria would certainly apply to employees who make a concerted effort to correct and improve their behavior after a difficult conversation.) The note should acknowledge the specific behavior that the leader wants to recognize, because as I've mentioned, specific behaviors that are recognized will be repeated. To get even more bang for your buck, you can mail the note to the employee or provider's home. This has the spinoff benefit of engaging the whole family and multiplying the understanding that the employee is appreciated and the organization is a great place to work.

When I talk to leadership groups about thank-you notes, I ask a series of questions and always get similar answers.

- *How old were you when you wrote your first thank-you note?* six

- *Who did you write the note to?* Grandmother

- *Why did you write the note?* Because my mother told me I had to

- *What was the note for?* A birthday present

- *What did you hope would result if you wrote the note?* I'd get a Christmas present.

The same thing is true in the work setting. If we are clear and specific with our employees about the behavior that is being recognized, it will be repeated.

Consequences are a valuable motivator and "teaching aid," but they should be employed only in conjunction with difficult conversations. Nothing will alienate and disengage your workforce faster than punishment without warning, explanation, or the opportunity to improve.

However, reward and recognition can and should be used independently of tough conversations. In fact, I encourage you to make "the two Rs" a general leadership practice. When you reward and recognize generously, the behaviors you are promoting will spread organically throughout your culture.

In time, the number of difficult conversations you need to have may decrease as people are inspired to positively adjust their behavior *without* the threat of consequences. That's truly a win-win!

CHAPTER EIGHT:

STANDARDS OF BEHAVIOR

I n several previous chapters, I have stated that Standards of Behavior can help you identify when a difficult conversation is necessary, conduct that conversation, and follow up on it. In this chapter, we'll look at what Standards of Behavior are and how they can support difficult conversations.

What Are Standards of Behavior?

Standards of Behavior are a set of official guidelines meant to govern employees' actions, speech, attitudes, and more. How do Standards of Behavior differ from typical organizational policies and Codes of Conduct? Instead of being phrased in terms of corporate goals, desired outcomes, and general dos and don'ts, standards describe specific desired behaviors.

They can cover any and all aspects of your workplace: from interactions with patients to phone etiquette to "good manners" (knocking on doors) to "positive attitude" markers (smiling or saying "thank you"). In other words, Standards of

Behavior tend to be quite detailed and "personalized." They are often created by the employees and not handed down from the C-suite. (That said, standards can and should still support your organization's overarching, long-term goals.)

A Sampling of Standards

Here are just a few examples of standards used at Studer Group® and other healthcare organizations. (As you'll see, there isn't a set format for standards. Some resemble policies; others read like personal pledges.):

- Maintain a high level of competency and the credentials required to provide the highest level of care possible.

- I will be the "voice with a smile" in person, on the phone, and via email communication.

- I will show a true sense of teamwork by setting aside personal differences in the name of excellent patient care.

- I will explain the expected duration of procedures, visits, and delays to patients.

- Keep public areas neat and clean—if the trash needs to be emptied, empty it.

- I will acknowledge your presence, introduce myself, and explain in a timely manner aspects related to your care.

- Do not send excessive emails—please place only those who are directly related to the issue or those you would like a response from in the "To" line. If you would like to inform someone of the issue and do not want a response, please "cc" them. Send your response emails within 24 hours only to the person sending the note unless it is necessary or asked for all to read your response.

- I will respect cultural, religious, and social backgrounds.

- Use adult conversations to resolve issues—go directly to the coworker involved.

- Welcome, mentor, and receive new team members with energy and "What can I do for you?" spirit.

- I will wear my ID badge where it can easily be seen.

- I will protect the confidentiality of our patients' privacy both in and out of the hospital.

- When on-site at an organization, always turn off cell phone and do not use partner's time for other business.

- Do not embarrass or criticize partners/co-workers in the presence of others.

Let's hear from one of my Studer Group colleagues, Bob Murphy. Bob has excellent insights on why standards are so valuable (and I couldn't say it any better!):

Most organizations have a set of standards in place they require staff to demonstrate and follow. But do we spend enough time focusing on their importance? Our research tells us that those organizations that truly live their Standards of Behavior every day achieve better results. The senior leaders, managers, and directors (and, ideally, all staff) understand and use the Standards of Behavior in everyday conversation. They become a part of their language so much so that they don't even realize they are using those words or practicing those behaviors.

Standards of Behavior offer staff guidelines to demonstrate the same level of behavior on a daily basis. They serve as a commitment to how we will treat each other and those we interact with. They are so important to setting the tone of the organization that we recommend posting them for visitors to see. This further demonstrates the value those standards have to our organization.

Every organization is different, and yet, the common thread still remains that the standards are in place not only to make the organization better, but to provide the best possible care to our patients.

You can find resources to help create and implement Standards of Behavior on Studer Group's website: www.studergroup.com.

How Do Standards of Behavior Support Tough Conversations?

Tough conversations are most effective—and easiest to conduct—when both people understand why the conversation was initiated, why the behavior being discussed is important, and what changes need to be made. Standards of Behavior provide a "shared language" that makes mutual understanding possible. They also provide a level playing field that allows all employees—not just leaders—to recognize and address behaviors that don't align with the organization's goals and values.

Often, you'll be able to reference a standard in difficult conversations. For instance, "When you agreed to our organization's Standards of Behavior, you promised to return emails as soon as possible, and always within 24 hours." Because the other person is already familiar with this standard, you do not need to explain what's wrong with not returning emails promptly, and why the behavior needs to change. Instead of a lengthy explanation or argument, your conversation is a simple reminder.

As I pointed out in Chapter 5, referencing a standard is sometimes the most effective way to coach someone (particularly a low performer). An employee who is inclined to disregard what they see as a suggestion or opinion will often react differently when reminded, "You signed a pledge to adhere to our standards, and the behavior I just saw violates our standard to always greet patients."

Best of all, keeping Standards of Behavior "front and center" in your organization will infuse them into your culture over time. (We'll look at several ways to make sure your staff members are living the standards later in the chapter.) When everyone knows and understands your standards, and sees them consistently modeled by leaders and colleagues, these behaviors will become second nature—and the overall need for difficult conversations will be reduced!

How Do I Use Standards of Behavior in Tough Conversations?

The more specific your organization's standards are and the better versed you are in them, the easier you'll find it to conduct tough conversations. (Yes, I'm using "easier" as a relative term here!) As I have said, when you are able to identify the Standard of Behavior that has been broken, describe the impact noncompliance has, and coach the other person on what needs to change, most of the "heavy lifting" for the conversation has already been done.

It's important to initiate a conversation about Standards of Behavior the first time you see an infraction. (Otherwise you are getting into permit/promote territory, which we'll discuss in Chapter 10.) Here are examples of how you can use Standards of Behavior to facilitate difficult conversations, using each of the three conversational models:

A Stub Your Toe Conversation with a high or solid/middle performer who isn't following a standard and would sound like this:

- Validate that the team member demonstrates positive behaviors, is good with patients, is a big help to coworkers, etc.

- "Suzy, do you remember signing our Standards of Behavior when you were hired? Do you remember that one of the standards is Commitment to Coworkers (or Responsiveness)? What does that mean to you?"

- Pause

- "Do you realize that every time you walk by a call light/ fail to pick up the phone/don't respond to an e-mail within our 24-hour standard, you are breaking a promise you made when you signed those standards?"

- Pause

- "I'm glad you understand the importance of our standards. That's what makes our culture here at XYZ great, but the culture depends on each of us role modeling those standards every day."

- "Thanks for your time. Now let's get back to the floor/ department and put those great skills you have to work."

Sometimes, the simple Stub Your Toe Conversation isn't enough and needs to be reinforced with an Impact Message Conversation:

- "Suzy, *when you* walk by a patient room without noting that the call light is on, you are violating one of our Standards of Behavior."

- "*The result is* that a patient in need is not receiving the care they want."

- "*I need to have you* view every call light on the floor as an opportunity to respond to a patient who needs our assistance. No one should walk by a call light. That's a commitment we've all made."

- "*Can you do that?*"

When improvements aren't seen and the standard's violation continues, it's time to get your supervisor and your Human Resources partner involved so that you can move into Low Performer Conversation mode. Here's what that interaction might sound like:

- "Suzy, we need to have a serious conversation. I just saw you walk by a patient room without noting the call light. You know that always responding promptly to patient call lights is one of the Standards of Behavior you agreed to. Failure to comply can put patients at risk, and also places an unnecessary burden on your coworkers."

- "I am disappointed because even though we've talked about this before, your performance has not changed."

- "Tomorrow, I have asked Bill to shadow you. He will give you tips on how to respond promptly to call lights while also accomplishing all of your other tasks within your scheduled shift. Please accept his coaching in the spirit in which it's intended—we simply want to help you shift your behavior to provide the best possible care to patients and we believe you want this, too."

- "Going forward, I will review your work each day and will give you feedback on adhering to this important standard. We will meet formally this time next week. If your performance has not improved, we will need to move to the first step in our disciplinary process. Do you understand the importance of adhering to the Standards of Behavior you agreed to practice? Do you understand my expectations moving forward? Do you have any questions?"

How Can I Ensure That Employees Consistently Live the Standards?

Standards of Behavior won't be very effective in difficult conversations (and in transforming your overall culture) if they are just a poster on the wall or a paper employees signed in orientation. As I said earlier, it is vital that standards be a living, breathing part of your organization. Here are some tactics to keep standards top of mind at all times:

- Most organizations introduce new employees or providers to the standards when they apply for a position or for credentialing. This way, there is absolutely no question that all employees have entered your organization with a clear understanding of the behaviors that are expected of them. Anyone who does not feel that they can adhere to your standards should not proceed with their application. After an employee is hired, standards should be highlighted once again at orientation.

- Make sure that everyone in your organization is held accountable. If some team members are allowed to ignore or flout certain standards, the organization's entire culture will suffer. Furthermore, the standards will not be taken seriously. (Again, this is why it is so important to have the appropriate difficult conversation as soon as you observe a violation.)

- Choose one standard to highlight each month. For instance, you might:

    ° Have leaders describe what the standard means to them.

    ° Talk about the *why* behind each standard at departmental meetings.

    ° Discuss the standard at huddles and ask team members to share stories of what that standard looks like in their daily work.

    ° Have a challenge, activity, or other event based around the monthly standard to make it fun. For example, if the featured standard is about the dress code, hold a fashion show to demonstrate what is and isn't appropriate. If it's about a safety issue, ask each team to create a public service announcement poster or hold a door decorating contest.

- Regularly reward and recognize employees who are role modeling the standards. (See Chapter 7 for more information on rewards and recognition.)

- Incorporate standards into each staff member's annual evaluation. You might even consider evaluating the employee based on how well they live out each of the standards. Simply list your organization's standards and place a yes/no option next to each. If an employee is living and role modeling a particular standard, circle "yes." If not, circle "no" and put that person on a disciplinary, performance, or coaching plan. A continued pattern of "noes" signals a low performer who should be moved out of the organization. It's unacceptable for someone to habitually fail to comply with the organizational standards and continue their employment.

• Post your standards publicly where visitors, patients, and/or customers can see them. Employees will be even more motivated to consistently be on their "best behavior" when they know that patients will be aware of noncompliance—and that a patient complaint could spark a difficult conversation!

What About "Non-Employees"?

Occasionally, your campus might host workers who are not "officially" on your payroll and/or who did not go through your hiring process. These might include temps, volunteers, registry staff, and contractors who are building or repairing facilities. Since patients, families, and visitors don't differentiate between "your" employees and others who are working in your facilities, it is important to make sure that *every-one* complies with the Standards of Behavior. Therefore, abiding by your standards should be part of any contract your facility has with an agency or contractor.

Standards of Behavior are not absolutely necessary in order to talk to an employee about a change that needs to be made, but they certainly make these conversations easier to initiate, carry out, and follow up on.

Once your organization develops Standards of Behavior, don't allow them to be "just" words on a piece of paper. Make them a part of each team member's everyday vocabulary and actions. By conducting training, using rewards and recognition, and applying consequences when a conversation about noncompliance doesn't result in change, you can ensure that positive behaviors do, in fact, become "the golden standard."

CHAPTER NINE:

DIFFICULT CONVERSATIONS WITH PHYSICIANS

E very time I lead a session about mastering tough
conversations, someone invariably asks, "But what about
the docs?" There's a general feeling that having a tough conversation with a physician has to be different from conversations with coworkers, employees, and other peers. But that's
just not true! And placing physicians in a different category
from other employees isn't the most productive way to view
your culture.

Think about it from this perspective: Our providers are
no strangers to tough conversations. Many physicians initiate
difficult conversations every day! Sometimes those conversations are with a patient who has an incurable disease or isn't
following their treatment plan. Sometimes the conversation is
with their medical assistant or front desk staffer who is dressed
inappropriately, always on their personal cell phone, or acting
snarly toward a coworker when patients are around.

My point is, physicians understand why tough conversations are necessary. Moreover, they are working toward the
same overarching goal that you are: providing the highest-
quality experience possible for patients. Like the majority of

employees in your organization, most physicians will ultimately appreciate the fact that you took the time to talk to them about a behavior that needs to change. Conducted correctly and with compassion, the three conversational models can help bring your entire team closer together.

If possible, your physician leaders should be included in the training you are doing on difficult conversation models. As you cascade any of these models to all staff, certainly include your providers.

Leaders Are Team Members, Too

While this chapter focuses on having difficult conversations with physicians, many of the insights shared apply to conversations with leaders too. Similarly to how they view physicians, many employees tend to place their leaders in a separate category. They assume that tough conversations with leaders should be conducted differently or avoided altogether. Again, that's not true. As long as your intent is to strengthen your culture and improve the patient experience (as opposed to say "gotcha!" to the boss), you can use Stub Your Toe Conversations and Impact Messages to address concerning behaviors. Keep in mind, though, that Low Performer

> Conversations should always be delivered by the offender's own leader, since disciplinary procedures may follow.

What About the Exceptions to the Rule?

When someone asks, "What about the docs?" they are most likely referring to the stereotypical rude, abrasive, dysfunctional provider whom we see on TV. You know, the one who is yelling, screaming, or throwing things; demeaning the nurse; or not offering an explanation when giving the patient and family bad news. Fortunately, the majority of physicians I've encountered in "real life" strive to be good team members and would not dream of behaving in this manner, even on a bad day. I'm sure you've had the same experience.

That said, there *are* exceptions to every rule. If a "stereotypical TV doc"—even a somewhat toned-down version—works at your organization, it is crucial that you address this unacceptable behavior. Threatening, intimidating, and otherwise disruptive behavior in hospitals endangers patient safety, according to The Joint Commission on Accreditation of Healthcare Organizations (JCAHO). (And it doesn't matter if the tantrum-thrower is a physician or an administrator.)

Your organization should have policies and procedures meant to address inappropriate physician behavior. A JCAHO leadership standard effective January 1, 2009, requires hospitals and other accredited organizations to adopt and implement a code of conduct that defines and manages disruptive or inappropriate behavior by physicians and administrators. Leadership Standard LD.03.01.01 was announced in Sentinel Event Alert 40 issued on July 9, 2008, entitled "Behaviors That Undermine a Culture of Safety."

Disruptive or inappropriate behavior patterns include:

- overt actions, such as verbal outbursts and physical threats

- passive activities, such as refusing to perform assigned tasks or quietly exhibiting uncooperative attitudes during routine activities

- reluctance or refusal to answer questions, return phone calls or pages

- condescending language or voice intonation and impatience with questions

The three conversational models in this book can be very helpful in your organization's efforts to address, document, and manage these behaviors. Keep in mind that if a physician's behavior does not change after more than one conversation, they are a low performer—and should be moved out of the organization if further disciplinary procedures do not have an effect.

My California colleague Alan Rosenstein, MD, has researched, published about, and speaks extensively on disruptive and inappropriate behaviors. Why is this so important to address? Dr. Rosenstein's research validates that when we don't address the behavior, the patient may die!

Use Codes of Conduct to Define Appropriate Physician Behavior—and Support Difficult Conversations

As mentioned in Chapter 8, Standards of Behavior facilitate (and over time, reduce the need for) difficult conversations. All physicians should sign the hospital's Standards of Behavior, especially if they are organizational employees. (It's also helpful to make standards part of the credentialing process—this way, every provider's commitment to standards must be renewed each time they are recredentialed.)

Beyond Standards of Behavior, it's also wise to ask your organization's providers to develop their own code of conduct covering behaviors specific to their role in the organization. Issue #4 of Studer Group's *Hardwired Results®* magazine (published in 2005) explains what a physician code of conduct is and why it's important. Here are some relevant excerpts from that article:

In our experience, hospitals that serve physicians well create loyal physicians who manage up nurses, submit excellent ideas for operational improvement, and reward and recognize high performing staff. When they see what a difference standards of conduct make for employees, they even create their own standards...

Every organization does it differently. Some organizations ask physicians to sign the same standards their employees follow. Others use professional standards based on provisions of the medical staff bylaws, rules, and regulations. And some are very prescriptive and specific to physicians.

"Our standards were created by physicians for physicians," explains Dr. Stephen Beeson, formerly of Sharp Rees-Stealy Medical Group (affiliated with Sharp HealthCare in San Diego, CA), who rolled out the

standards to the group's 700 physicians. "Physicians were asked to sign a pledge that says they commit to promote a positive workplace environment for staff and fellow physicians through specific behaviors."

When they sign the pledge, Sharp Rees-Stealy physicians agree to return patient phone calls and pages promptly, work cooperatively with staff and nurses, submit charges for services provided in a timely fashion, and communicate in a respectful way, among other things. An accompanying "Physician Code" expresses Sharp Rees-Stealy Medical Group's vision of what excellent physician leadership looks like and why it is important: to offer quality services that set community standards and exceed expectations in a caring, convenient, affordable, and accessible manner.

The code explains that the medical group seeks to create ideals that define the type of physician who works there and to provide an atmosphere where physicians flourish professionally and personally. Having connected to purpose, the code then details expected physician behaviors with respect to staff, physician colleagues, and patients…

"Physicians are no different than anyone else," adds Dr. Loren Meyer of All Saints Healthcare in Racine, WI. "We expect them to treat everyone with respect and dignity. I find that those who already do so don't have a problem signing standards." All Saints routinely takes action with non-compliant physicians, even removing an exclusive contract for clinical services in one case. Employed physicians are awarded incentive compensation based on patient satisfaction and peer/staff feedback.

If your organization already has a physician code of conduct or decides to create one, you can use it similarly to Standards of Behavior when conducting difficult conversations and coaching physicians. When a physician is reminded of a pledge they signed and why it is important, that physician will most likely be motivated to change their behavior for the good of the team and the organization—and most of all, for the good of the patients.

A Physician's Perspective on Difficult Conversations

To help get clearer insight on conducting difficult conversations with physicians, I sat down with Jeff Morris, MD, who is a physician leader and Studer Group coach. With more than 30 years of clinical practice and 12 years of physician executive leadership, Jeff has great perspective.

Get to Know Dr. Morris

Dr. Jeff Morris is a board-certified orthopedic & hand surgeon (Canada) who has lived and practiced in Ohio for the past 24 years. Originally from South Africa, he completed residencies there, in Israel, and a third residency and fellowship at Queen's University, Kingston, Ontario. He practiced in Thunder Bay and Burlington, Ontario, before moving to the U.S. in 1990. He completed his MBA at Kent State University in 2000 and later gained certification in medical acupuncture. Dr. Morris still maintains a part-time practice in non-surgical orthopedics and medical acupuncture.

Having spent 12 years as the vice president of medical affairs (VPMA) in two community hospitals and in Summa Health System in Northeast Ohio, Dr. Morris served as the internal physician champion and helped to elevate the culture of service and enhance communications at these facilities. His efforts resulted in a significant improvement in physician and employee engagement, as well as elevation of the patients' perception of the quality of care being delivered—a big advantage, with so many healthcare competitors in the local market.

Dr. Morris joined Studer Group as a physician coach in 2010, sharing his passion for servant leadership, service excellence, and improving the patient experience. He has worked with many physicians and medical staff leaders, both local and across the country, to "connect these dots." Dr. Morris also teaches healthcare marketing in the Kent State University Healthcare Executive MBA Program, serves as an independent medical examiner, and has coauthored a number of books.

Dr. Morris's overall advice for having tough conversations with physicians is short, straight, and direct: "It's not really different from any other conversation. You've got to start with the physician's *what* and then connect the dots to the purpose of your conversation and talk about how behavior impacts the work environment and clinical outcomes." To that end, he says that it's usually productive to start the conversation by saying, "Let's talk about why this is important."

Read on for a more in-depth look at what I asked Dr. Morris during our conversation and what I learned:

Can all three models for mastering tough conversations be used with physicians? Dr. Morris says, "YES!" As you know, the Stub Your Toe Conversation is ideal when you see or hear something that is inconsistent with the code of conduct or Standards of Behavior. The Impact Message is ideal for reinforcing the physician's *what* and *why*. The Low Performer Conversation is appropriate in an employed physician model.

Remember that before having any type of difficult conversation, it's important to build an emotional or trust "bank account" by ensuring that physicians receive appropriate positive feedback and reward/recognition when they deserve it. Of course, the tough conversation itself should always be focused on the patient, high-quality care, and how to improve in this realm.

Who is the best person to have the conversation? If you want to have an impact, the *right person* needs to have the conversation with the physician. Although anyone with the appropriate skills can have a tough conversation with a physician, the conversation will probably go most smoothly if the person initiating the conversation is respected by the physician. This could be the chief medical officer or chief of service, but it could also be a physician champion, department manager, nurse leader, or staff nurse who has a positive relationship with the physician and who understands the physician's *what*. Being familiar with the organization's Standards of Behavior and the medical staff's code of conduct is crucial.

How can you connect the conversation to a physician's *what*? Is the physician resistant to following a standardized protocol? If the physician's *what* is "quality," then point out that evidence shows that compliance with standardized protocols positively affects clinical outcomes.

Is the physician using AIDET® inconsistently? If the physician's *what* is "efficiency" of practice or "time management," then talk about the importance of setting time expectations (the "D" in AIDET) and "managing up" (the "I" in AIDET).

Dr. Morris notes, "It's common sense. It's like treating a patient. You don't treat every patient with the same diagnosis in the same way. You have to determine how you will be most impactful and who will have the most influence in each situation. Then determine the message you need to send and how best to communicate it."

What about the physician who isn't following the code of conduct or your Standards of Behavior? "First make sure that others are following the code and being held to the same standard," Dr. Morris recommends. "Then ask, does the policy, standard, or code make sense? If it doesn't make sense anymore, change the code. It doesn't inspire compliance to have a code or standards that are out-of-date and aren't being followed consistently. It needs to be the right thing and the smart thing to do.

"It's also important to get to the *real* root of the problem," notes Dr. Morris. "I once needed to have a conversation with a physician who was coming up on our quality reports as someone with multiple late starts in the operating room.

However, when I looked further at the data, I learned that part of the reason that he was starting late was because of numerous other factors that were beyond his control—like the rooms weren't ready or the patient arrived late. The worst thing one can do is approach a physician with the wrong data. The best thing one can do is make it easy for the physician to do the right thing."

Dr. Morris makes a good point here. Often there are infrastructural issues that get in the way of high performers' ability to do their jobs, causing them to "stub their toe." To maintain the confidence of the medical staff, you need to commit to studying the infrastructure issue and seeing if barriers to "doing the right thing" can be removed.

A final word of advice from Dr. Morris on this point: "During recredentialing, have every physician reaffirm the code of conduct by signing it again during the reapplication process. And reappointment to the medical staff should not be a 'passive' action for the physician. The board should offer the physician reappointment, and the physician should recommit to the medical staff bylaws and code of conduct by 'actively' signing acceptance of the reappointment." As mentioned earlier in the chapter, this strategy also works well for Standards of Behavior—make them part of credentialing, recredentialing, and reappointment.

What is the best way to build the kind of positive relationship that facilitates tough conversations? It's just like working with your employees and it comes down to building trust. Start with rounding on physicians. Ask about what's working well, whom to reward and recognize, and opportunities for improvement. Chiefs and vice chiefs should be rounding on their department physicians. Don't create artificial barriers between employed and independent docs. Rounding provides a foundation for building trust and developing the relationship—and that is important for all clinicians.

How should you proceed if physicians are involved in a triangulated conversation? Doctors can be guilty of triangulating tough conversations just like anyone else. Dr. Morris notes, "When I was a VPMA, there were a couple of physicians in one department who were rude, dysfunctional, and chauvinistic. Another physician (from the same department) complained at a department meeting about something one of the dysfunctional docs did when on the floor. Unfortunately the doc who came to talk to me didn't say anything to the offending colleague at the time he witnessed the unacceptable behavior—he just complained later to the VPMA! Instead of me talking to the offending physician, my response was to coach the complaining doctor on how to have the conversation with his colleague at the time this occurred, explaining how much more effective this would be in positively changing his colleague's behavior than a scolding from someone who heard about it secondhand."

What if the physician doesn't respond positively? Even for a physician, it's uncomfortable when someone has a tough conversation with them. Physicians have feelings too, and it's hard for them to be on the receiving end of a Stub Your Toe, Impact Message, or Low Performer Conversation. Just like any other employee, a physician might initially react with resistance, denial, or by trying to justify the behavior. And just like any other employee, after they've had time to think about what you discussed, most physicians will realize that a behavior change *is* needed to support your shared mission of making patients' lives better.

What if the first conversation doesn't result in the desired change in behavior? Your code of conduct and medical staff bylaws should give you guidance on what next steps to take. However, in order to avoid accusations of "discriminatory discipline," you need to ensure that there is consistent enforcement of these standards.

What if the behavior is egregious? That's when a formal physician leader needs to get involved, and, as before, medical staff bylaws should give you guidance on what steps to take.

Dr. Morris's advice works equally well in the hospital or outpatient setting and serves Dr. Morris well as a physician coach. He makes the point that "communication isn't just about delivering the message; it's also necessary for the person receiving the message to be receptive to the message." So analyze the situation, pick the best person to deliver the message, and use the appropriate model to have the necessary tough conversation.

Remember, while physicians hold a prominent position in any healthcare organization, they are also members of the overall team. Treat them as such—in positive *and* difficult conversations—and you will ultimately strengthen your culture, reinforce your Standards of Behavior, and make the patient experience the best it can be.

PART THREE:

BARRIERS TO TOUGH CONVERSATIONS

CHAPTER TEN:

WHAT WE PERMIT, WE PROMOTE

As I speak with audiences across the country about having tough conversations, I find that it's typically not the BIG things that cause people to hesitate about initiating a difficult conversation. It's the seemingly little things.

What do I mean by "little things"? Well, recall that in Chapter 5 I discussed the need to evaluate employees on two scales: job competencies and adherence to our Standards of Behavior. (Refer back to Figure 5.6 if you'd like a refresher.) We normally don't have any trouble coaching and disciplining the person who just can't master the basics of the job—even if they're really nice. *Especially* in healthcare, job competencies just aren't something we can compromise on.

However, we *do* have trouble initiating difficult conversations that revolve around standards, policies, and values. We're deeply reluctant to confront the skilled nurse, busy surgeon, or industrious housekeeper who doesn't follow the dress code, uses their cell phone on the job, consistently clocks in seven minutes late, smokes on campus, or ignores requests for information. *This person is so good at the things that* really *matter,* we tell ourselves. *I don't want to make them mad and risk causing their performance to decline, so I'll just keep my mouth shut about this little issue.*

But here's the thing: Every time we ignore those "little" issues, we are basically saying, "It's okay. You're one of our MVPs, so you don't have to follow all the rules. You're still a great employee."

No, they aren't!

"Great employee" is another way of saying "high performer." If your organization has a standard, policy, or code of conduct and someone is not compliant with "the rules," they aren't a high performer—period. If you've talked to them before and the behavior hasn't changed, they aren't even a solid/middle performer. They are a low performer and should be on a performance plan, regardless of their clinical skill.

Don't forget that the rest of your staff is watching. They hear you saying—with your actions, if not with your words—"It's okay. Go ahead and break the rules." If you don't stop an inappropriate behavior the first time you see it, others will think you've changed the rules and will assume that it's okay for them to no longer comply.

Rules Are There for a Reason

If something is part of "the rules," then enforce the rule. If it's a bad rule or needs to be changed because the times have changed, then change it. But whatever you do, *don't* ignore those who are breaking a rule that's in place for a reason.

Words of Wisdom: "What You Permit, You Promote"

Studer Group has a great little exercise I love to do with groups called "permit/promote." It's low-tech, so you can do it at a team meeting or department huddle, as well as at a Leadership Development Institute.

If you're not familiar with this exercise, let me share an explanation from the master himself. In 2007, Quint Studer wrote the following blog post titled "What You Permit, You Promote."

Liz Jazwiec and I have been colleagues for more than 10 years. We first met at Holy Cross Hospital in Chicago, IL. Liz is a great presenter and a difference maker. My favorite thing I learned from Liz is, "What you permit, you promote."

When I became president of a hospital in 1996, 23 percent of employees had late evaluations. I became aware of this issue when I mentioned to some employees our organization's value of respect. An employee said, "*If we are so respected, why is my evaluation late?*" Thus, my search led me to find that 23 percent of our employees were waiting for an evaluation to be completed and some had been waiting for weeks and months. If an employee's evaluation was late, nothing happened to the leader who did not complete it by the deadline.

I guaranteed all staff that in 60 days there would be no late evaluations. I put in systems and consequences, positive recognition to leaders with no late evaluations, and connected the dots on why an on-time evaluation is crucial to show staff respect and retain employees. Sixty days later, there were no late evaluations nor were there any while I was there. I believe the system of on-time evaluations and results is still strong.

A few years back, we had a meeting with Studer Group staff members and posed the following question: "*What are we permitting, thus promoting?*" When people are asked that question, one will hear some good feedback and some ways to improve. For example, one may hear, "*You are permitting us to hire our coworkers, thus promoting responsibility and ownership for new hires.*" We also heard that we needed to do a better job walking the talk in some areas, and this caused us to tighten up. While the journey was not comfortable, it was worthwhile and made us better.

In our travels, we find that many organizations are not fully aware of what they are permitting, thus promoting. Here are some examples:

- *A leader who consistently is not meeting patient satisfaction goals* [Aside: In today's context, this might be HCAHPS, CG CAHPS, or another formal survey you are using.] *is not dealt with, or worse yet, still gets a good review. We are promoting poor performance.*

- *A vice president who is not sharing information that others are sharing. We are permitting inconsistent communication.*

- *Staff not following agreed-upon and signed Standards of Behavior (performance). We are permitting staff to not live the behaviors agreed upon, thus hurting the organizational results.*

- *Allowing a physician to intimidate staff. We know from research that if staff is scared, they may not address patient issues with the physician. By allowing intimidation, we are not providing staff or patients the safest environment.*

- *A leader keeps blaming the data for results. We are permitting, thus promoting, excuses.*

- *A person is on his or her BlackBerry* [Aside: In today's context, that would be an iPhone or another personal electronic device.] *during a meeting. We are permitting lack of respect, thus promoting lack of attention.*

You get the gist of it.

Ask yourself: "What am I permitting, thus promoting?" At your meeting, put on the agenda: "What are we permitting, thus promoting?" At the next department head meeting, take some time to ask leaders what they feel the senior leaders are permitting, thus promoting. At your next staff meeting, ask staff what is being permitted, thus promoted. While you may be disappointed in what you hear, you will not be disappointed in the opportunities presented to improve the organization or the outcomes that will be achieved.

Once you address what you are promoting, leaders may feel they need more training. It may be that at times leaders permit things because they do not know how to handle them.

When conducting the permit/promote exercise, feel free to use some of the examples from Quint's blog post. Another option is to give small groups of team members two minutes to

brainstorm what they see being permitted within your department or organization that shouldn't be. I think you'll be surprised by how quickly they identify permit/promote examples.

Harvest those examples and get a commitment from the
team that these behaviors will not be tolerated going forward.
You'll be glad you took this step…and so will your patients.

Difficult Conversations Ensure That You *Don't* Permit What You Wouldn't Promote: Six Examples

Even when you know it's the right thing to do, confronting
someone about a permit/promote situation is easier said than
done. For the remainder of this chapter, let's look at examples
of how the three tough conversations models can be used to
address permit/promote observations.

Example 1: Employee Evaluations Are Late. First,
let's delve into one of the examples Quint used in his blog post.
This situation is ideal for the Impact Message Conversation,
since it is an ongoing occurrence and leaders may need to be
reminded of how their tardiness affects their teams.

- *"When you* fail to complete your employee evaluations on
  time…"

- *"The result is* that employees feel you don't respect them
  and the work they do."

- *"Because employee engagement is a key goal we share,* it is critical
  that timely employee evaluations are a priority for all of
  us."

- "*I need to have you* conform strictly to the established deadlines for completing employee evaluations so we can consistently communicate our value of respect to each employee."

- "*Do you agree* to meet these deadlines in the future?"

Example 2: An Employee Is Smoking on Campus. Many of the permit/promote situations you will encounter are violations of standards or policies that you personally witness. A Stub Your Toe Conversation is appropriate.

- "Sam, you're doing an excellent job with the new assignment in environmental services. I'm hearing very positive feedback from nursing leaders when I round with them. They appreciate your attention to details in the patients' rooms and in the public areas on the nursing unit."

- "I would like to remind you that our facility has a campus-wide no smoking policy that applies to all employees, contract workers, and visitors. The policy was adopted to protect everyone's health and safety. I know that we sometimes see visitors smoking outside the hospital, but as employees we must set an example. That's why I was disappointed when I saw you smoking on the dock this morning." *(Pause and give Sam time for reflection.)*

- "Keep up the good work on the nursing unit. You always do a very thorough job and I'm proud of your performance. And remember to role model our no smoking policy."

Examples 3, 4, and 5: An Employee Is Habitually Tardy. What happens when you encounter a permit/promote situation and have the necessary conversation—but nothing changes? It is your responsibility to move to the next step in the coaching process—and to continue following up until the issue is resolved. If at any point you say to yourself, *Well, I tried to correct the behavior and it didn't work. I give up,* you are *still* permitting (and thus tacitly promoting) the undesirable behavior.

The following three examples show a progression from a Stub Your Toe Conversation all the way to a Low Performer Conversation.

First, you might have a Stub Your Toe Conversation with the employee:

- "Suzy, when you are on the job, you do excellent work. Your interactions with patients and your providers are always friendly and professional."

- "We have talked about your timeliness before, so I am concerned that you still don't arrive for the beginning of your shift every day. Do you know what you need to do to be prompt every day for every shift?"

- "Let's keep up the good work with patients and providers while respecting your coworkers and being on time."

If the employee does not improve and is habitually late, move on to an Impact Message Conversation:

- "*When you* are consistently late for your shift…"

- "*The result is* that you inconvenience your coworkers who can't leave on time. They incur overtime, which has a negative financial impact on the department and the organization."

- *"Your coworkers and I need you* to be prompt for every shift, every day."

- "You need to plan ahead so you are consistently on time. *Can you commit to that?"*

When these approaches have failed, it's time to move to the Low Performer Conversation:

- "Suzy, it's time for a very serious conversation."

- "We talked three times in the last month about your tardiness, so I'm sure you realize this behavior is not acceptable."

- "You know that you are expected to clock in on time every day."

- "I know you know where the time clock is and what your schedule is, yet you continue to be tardy on a regular basis."

- "I will be checking your time card on a daily basis starting tomorrow. If you continue to be tardy, I will need to initiate the next step in the disciplinary process, which can lead to suspension or dismissal. You have a choice to make and you need to make it quickly. If you want to continue working for us, you must be on time for your shifts."

Example 6: A Leader Is Consistently Missing a Critical Goal.

- "Tony, you know your patient satisfaction goal is a critical one for the organization. As the nursing leader of one of our largest units, your patients' perception of the care they are receiving impacts our facility scores and our value-based purchasing reimbursement."

- "Over the last six months, you have received group and personal coaching on the evidence-based skills that can positively impact your patients' satisfaction, yet there have been few improvements in your overall marks."

- "It's time we had a very serious conversation about your inability to achieve this goal. Remember, you participated in setting these goals and felt you could achieve the targets. I've made sure you received the resources and coaching you requested and still your patients' perceptions are in the lower quartile. Is there anything else you feel you need in order to be able to achieve the necessary progress?"

- "If not, I think it's time we look at an appropriate transition plan to move you to a position where you can be successful and to select another leader who will be able to achieve this critical goal. I want to continue this discussion with you next week. At that time, I want to hear a specific plan on what you will be doing daily in the next month to start making progress on this goal. If positive movement starts, we'll continue to monitor and support your actions. If not, we'll start the transition discussion. Am I clear? Do you have any questions?"

There's no doubt about it—these conversations are tough. It's easy to avoid them when you have other priorities. But who is the victim when we permit a behavior instead of confronting it? It's our patients, of course, and our employees and providers who *are* doing the right thing.

If you wouldn't actively promote a behavior, don't tacitly permit it—no matter how "little" it seems. Yes, skipping a difficult conversation might be easier or more comfortable in the short run, but you can be sure that this decision will have long-term negative consequences for your organization. So speak up!

CHAPTER ELEVEN:

LET'S STOP BULLYING

B ullying is not limited to the playground days of our youth. The same behaviors we feared in the schoolyard can also be found in our healthcare offices, departments, nursing units, and surgery suites today.

According to a study published in the *Journal of Management Studies*, bullying is defined as:

- At least two negative acts weekly (or more often) for six or more months

- Situations where targets feel it is difficult to defend against or stop the abuse[1]

If you're thinking that bullying doesn't happen in your organization, think again. Workplace bullying is more widespread than you may realize. According to the Workplace Bullying Institute, 35 percent of Americans report being bullied at work.[2] Furthermore, one 2014 survey of 400 leaders (39 percent from healthcare) found that 94 percent of respondents worked with a toxic person. The research identified three types of toxic behaviors: shaming, passive hostility, and team sabotage.[3]

I'm sure you've witnessed each of these toxic behaviors over the course of your career. For example, a physician might snap at a nurse, "Why can't you ever find the right chart?" A nurse might make a new employee her target for belittling remarks, condescending language, and other forms of public humiliation. An office administrator might be short and uncommunicative with patients (yes, patients can be bullied too) or may roll her eyes at mistakes made by older, non-technology-savvy nurses.

Make no mistake—workplace bullying has consequences. When an employee is bullied, their morale, self-confidence, and commitment to the organization can all decrease. Forty-five percent of bullied employees report stress-related health issues.[4] Dr. Alan Rosenstein's research draws a correlation between disruptive behaviors (like bullying) and the occurrence of medical errors and compromised quality, adverse events, compromises in patient safety, and a contributing factor to patient mortality.[5, 6] Clearly, bullying is something we can't allow to continue.

Insight from Girl Scouts

As we all know, bullying often starts in childhood. Interpersonal behaviors learned in a child's formative years—whether they are positive or negative—often influence their behavior well into adulthood. That's why Girl Scouts of the U.S.A. has researched and addressed the bullying problem for years.

As the leading organization for girls and an advocate for developing girls' leadership abilities, Girl Scouts' bullying prevention programs help children build social and emotional skills so they can handle challenges constructively. The programs help girls demonstrate concern for others, exercise empathy, recognize and manage emotions, and make responsible decisions. Girl Scouts' research notes that almost one-third of students report being bullied at school, and that six out of ten teens witness bullying at least once a day.[7]

"Bullying is an epidemic," says Pam Saltenberger, retired CEO of Girl Scouts Heart of Central California Council. "Bullies don't have a self-perception of their behavior."

As we deal with adult bullies in our organizations, this is valuable insight to keep in mind. Often, bullies don't accurately perceive how their behavior is interpreted by others or the impact it has on their teams, patients, and organizations. It's up to us to identify bullying behaviors and coach offenders toward change.

What's the Best Way to Deal with Bullies?

Think of a colleague, coworker, physician, or leader who is a bully. What are your options for dealing with this person? Pam Saltenberger, retired CEO of Girl Scouts Heart of Central California Council, says, "You have three choices:

1. You join the bully and become another bully.

2. You get out and leave the employer.

3. You become a victim."

But if you want your organization to become better, stronger, and more effective, none of these choices is acceptable. We need to implement a fourth option in our organizations: Have a respectful conversation with the bully, ensure the bully holds up the mirror and sees their dysfunctional behavior for what it is, and get them to change the behavior. Our employees and patients are depending on us to do just that. If we don't, bullying will spread—and employee engagement, clinical quality, and patient satisfaction will all decrease. To put it bluntly, we *cannot afford* to be among the 62 percent of employers who ignore workplace bullying.[8]

In the healthcare workplace, Standards of Behavior can be one of your greatest assets in identifying and combating bullying behaviors. Most organizations' standards speak to "respect," "teamwork," or a similar value. Bullying is contrary to these standards, making it (relatively) easy to identify and its negative impact easy to describe. Furthermore, when an employee refuses to comply with a standard, your path to initiating disciplinary procedures is clear.

How Do I Talk to Bullies About Their Behavior?

Knowing how to use Studer Group's three models for mastering tough conversations can help stop the bullies in our organizations, even if the intimidation has gone on for years. Training our leaders and staff on how to put a stop to bullying can reduce employee turnover, increase employee satisfaction, and ensure that the organization's Standards of Behavior are followed and respected by all. Let's look at how each conversational model applies to bullying.

The Stub Your Toe Conversation is the best model to use when you have seen or heard bullying behavior that is inconsistent with the organization's standards or values, and that you have *not* witnessed on a recurring basis. Keeping in mind that the names below are tongue-in-cheek references to some healthcare professional stereotypes, the conversation might sound like this:

- "Nurse Frown, I so *value* your clinical skills and the way you care for your patients. You have great potential to impart this knowledge to our newer team members."

- "Earlier today when you were instructing Suzy New-Nurse on how to do a specific procedure for the first time, I *heard* you use a tone of voice that implied she was stupid or a slow learner. Suzy was embarrassed because this exchange occurred in front of one of her patients. I know you are familiar with our Standards of Respect and Teamwork. Since Suzy was not endangering the patient, it would have been preferable to wait until you were out of the patient's room and then provide the necessary coaching."

- *"Again, I want to emphasize that I respect* your clinical skills and think you have great potential to be a strong mentor and preceptor. You just need to remember that you, too, learned things as a new nurse, and need to use your best coaching skills when you work with others."

The Impact Message is ideal to use with colleagues, employees, or supervisors when a bullying behavior appears to be consistent and is disruptive to the organization. It could sound like this:

- "Dr. Snarl, *when you* yell and scream and use degrading language to one of the OR techs or a nurse on the floor…"

- *"The result is* they are intimidated and no longer want to work with you. They pull back and resist the clinical expertise you have and could impart to them. If you have a patient on their floor, they may become reluctant to call you when the patient is in distress. Research has shown that this can result in delayed care and even patient deaths."

- *"We all need you to* demonstrate our organizational Standards of Respect and Teamwork by communicating in a professional way with all members of the team. If you don't feel you are getting the cooperation or results you need, please come and speak to me [the supervisor] rather than exhibiting these inappropriate behaviors."

- *"Can you do this?"*

And finally, when initial conversations haven't been successful in stopping the bullying behavior, the Low Performer Conversation is necessary. The low performer is someone who consistently abuses organizational guidelines. Most likely, they are widely known throughout their team, department, or even the entire organization as being a bully.

- Remember, we don't start this conversation with any positive comments.

- "Nurse Ratched, the behavior I just *observed* was completely inappropriate. Your intimidating comments and disrespectful attitude had the scrub techs in the OR shaking with fear. Nancy even dropped an instrument she was preparing to hand to Dr. Jones."

- "I'm *disappointed* in you. We've had this conversation before and still this behavior continues on a regular basis."

- "The last time we talked, you *assured me* you could work with your teammates and communicate in a respectful manner. I don't see that the problem has been resolved."

- "Continuation of this behavior is unacceptable. Because you have not been able to perform within our Standards of Behavior, I will be *writing you up* for this occurrence. This is the first step in our formal disciplinary process. I expect your performance to change immediately. If it doesn't, the disciplinary process will proceed until you are able to consistently demonstrate this competency or you will be dismissed from your position."

With any of these conversations, follow-through is a must. When the other person moves toward compliance following a conversation, give them positive feedback the next time they demonstrate appropriate behavior: "Thank you for demonstrating the behavior that we discussed last week. I appreciate your follow-through."

And what if the behavior doesn't change? There needs to be follow-through here, too. Noncompliance, especially after a commitment to change has been made, must have consequences. This employee needs to be entered into the disciplinary process. Follow-up also needs to be constant until the behavior is appropriately changed.

Because The Joint Commission requires all medical staffs to create a code of conduct that defines acceptable and unacceptable behaviors and to establish a formal process for managing unacceptable behavior, I know that your organization has procedures in place for dealing with bullies. Again, make sure there is *persistent* and *consistent* follow-through to ensure that the behavior changes—it is all too common for leaders to permit (and thus promote) a return to undesirable behaviors after the initial conversation.

Two Perspectives on the Future of Bullying

While bullying remains widespread in healthcare workplaces, there is good news: It may become less and less common in the future. Here's what two experts have to say:

In his book *Unaccountable: What Hospitals Won't Tell You and How Transparency Can Revolutionize Health Care*, Marty Makary, MD, writes, "Thankfully there is a new generation of doctors and nurses moving up through the ranks with little tolerance for the immature behavior once modeled by the surgical elite. The current generation of health professionals signed up for medicine on the understanding that there are rules: rules for behavior, mutual respect, and rules limiting their work week to a more humane schedule. I am witnessing a generation eager to get at the root causes of our fragmented and uncoordinated system of care. Bad behavior is no longer swept under the rug."[9]

Pam Saltenberger, retired CEO of Girl Scouts Heart of Central California Council, agrees with Makary and muses, "As a younger generation is learning how to deal more effectively with bullying and is not willing to put up with this dysfunctional behavior, I think we will see more respect and collegiality in the workplace. We must start helping young people know how to deal with bullies on the playground so they will have appropriate coping skills as they mature and enter the workplace. It's incumbent upon us to call out bullies already in the workplace or we'll never be able to recruit and retain the most skilled and dedicated workers of the future."

Bullying—whether on the playground or in the workplace—is something we should all work to stop. With solid Standards of Behavior in place and a commitment from leadership to uphold these standards, you can use one or more of the difficult conversation models to address bullying when you see it. Remember, your goal is to get the bully to acknowledge their bullying behavior, and then to coach them on how to make a change—or invite them to "find their happiness elsewhere."

Your organization's employees and providers need to know that bullying behavior is unacceptable. Your patients are counting on you, too. Providing excellent patient care in a respectful, team-oriented environment depends on your ability to have these conversations and to hold staff and providers accountable for unacceptable behavior.

CHAPTER TWELVE:

TRIANGULATION

I f you look up "triangulation" on Wikipedia, this is what you learn: *Triangulation is a situation in which one family member will not communicate directly with another family member, but will communicate with a third family member, which can lead to the third family member becoming part of the triangle. The concept originated in the study of dysfunctional family systems, but can describe behaviors in other systems as well, including work.*

Sound familiar? In healthcare, many of us (employees, providers, and even veteran leaders!) are tempted to turn to triangulation when we encounter a situation that requires a difficult conversation. Instead of confronting the offender directly, we report the behavior or incident to a third party. Sometimes that third party is someone who is higher than the offender in the organizational structure, and who will be expected to deal with the issue. Other times, the third party is a coworker or colleague. The person who witnessed the incident doesn't expect their colleague to do anything about the situation—they just want to vent and complain.

There are just a few problems with this strategy. First, the detrimental behavior is not addressed promptly (and perhaps not ever). Secondly, triangulation encourages gossip and "he said, she said" conversations among people who were not involved in the original incident. For many reasons, this is bad for your culture—not least because it prevents employees from focusing on their work.

Sure, we feel better for a few minutes after we initiate triangulation because we've passed the buck, or simply because we've gotten our frustration off our chest. But often as not, the situation doesn't change. It lives another day to annoy us further.

Two Leaders on Triangulation

When the subject of triangulation comes up, I think immediately of Lynne Thomas Gordon, CEO of the American Health Information Management Association. (With over 101,000 members, AHIMA is the largest healthcare membership association in the country. It represents health information management professionals and coders in hospitals, medical offices, and related healthcare organizations.) Lynne Thomas Gordon thinks triangulation is a cancer infecting our organizations that has to be stopped. When she talks about triangulation, she takes the thumb and forefinger of each hand, puts the fingertips together and creates a triangle. Everyone on her team knows what's coming next: a strong reminder that triangulation doesn't benefit the organization or solve problems.

My former colleague Beth Keane (to whom this book is dedicated) called triangulation "sending mail to the wrong mailbox." When you talk to a colleague or supervisor about a problem instead of speaking directly to the offender, you are sending mail to the wrong mailbox.

Stop the Triangulation Train: Three Examples

First, let's look at three examples of how you can decide to have a difficult conversation yourself instead of initiating triangulation. At this point in the book, these sample scripts will be a review—but fortunately, a little review never hurt anyone! The more examples of difficult conversations you encounter, the better prepared you'll be.

Example 1: Jill is not following the dress code today. You might feel like complaining to a coworker ("Can you believe Jill wore that to work?")—but don't give in to the temptation. Instead, have a quick Stub Your Toe Conversation with Jill and remind her of the dress code. It is important to restate why the dress code exists: "Jill, we wear white slacks and dark blue scrub tops so our patients know that we are a nurse on their floor. It decreases confusion and even anxiety. I know you love Minnie Mouse, but you still need to comply with our standards and wear the right scrubs." You might suggest that Jill change into the right scrubs. If you're Jill's supervisor and see the offense, you may decide to send her home to change without pay.

- "Jill, it's always a pleasure to see your name on the schedule when I'm working. I know we can handle just about anything when we work as a team."

- "I know you're familiar with our dress code. The purpose of the dress code is to ensure we are all presenting a professional appearance to our patients and families. The dress code specifically spells out that nurses wear white slacks and dark blue tops or scrubs. Your Minnie Mouse top just doesn't present the professional appearance we want our patients to see, and it could confuse them on whether you should be providing them care."

- "Can I cover for you for five minutes while you go change into a scrub top?"

- "Thanks for understanding."

Example 2: John shows up late again for the safety meeting you chair. Don't roll your eyes and then talk to another committee member after the meeting about how frustrating John's tardiness is. Have an Impact Message Conversation with John and ensure he understands how his behavior is affecting others on the team.

- "John, *when you* consistently show up late for the safety meetings and then ask to be caught up on the conversation you've missed…"

- *"The result is* you disrupt the flow of the meeting and communicate the message to others that their time isn't valuable."

- "In the future, *I need* you to be on time for the meeting. If you can't do that because of a patient commitment, please come in quietly and I'll catch you up later."

- *"Do I have your commitment* to do that?"

Example 3: George continues to leave his work area messy at the end of his shift. He doesn't offer to help team members who are still busy with assignments after he has finished with his own work. As George's leader, you've talked to him several times about respect and commitment to coworkers—which are two of your standards—and he's been on a performance plan. Yet the behavior persists. Instead of rationalizing George's behavior to another leader or to your cat at home, it's time to talk to your Human Resources partner again and make sure you understand the progressive discipline process. If you haven't had a Low Performer Conversation with George, it's probably time that he is made aware of the consequences he is facing. Ensure that he understands your expectations and that another offense will result in additional corrective action—perhaps a suspension without pay.

- "George, I'm disappointed in your behavior that clearly violates our Standards of Respect and Commitment to Coworkers."

- "We've talked several times about the importance of leaving your work area clean and uncluttered and offering to help coworkers before the end of the shift when you are finished and they are still busy."

- "George, you have a decision to make. You can begin to role model our standards immediately or you will move to the next step in the progressive discipline process, which means that I will place you on a three-day suspension without pay. It's your choice."

Instead of Enabling Triangulation, Help Others Have Tough Conversations

Most of this book is dedicated to giving you the tools you need to avoid instigating triangulation yourself (i.e., mastering tough conversations). But what can you do when another employee brings a problem to you in order to avoid having a difficult conversation?

When someone comes to you complaining of a situation you didn't see or hear personally, don't facilitate triangulation. If at all possible, coach the individual coming to you on how to have a tough conversation with the other person. Let's look at how this might play out.

Sam has just reported an issue with his coworker Suzy to you. The best response when someone comes to you complaining of a third party is, "What did Suzy say when you talked to her about the behavior/problem?"

Your question will typically be answered with, "Oh, I can't talk to Suzy. She gets too emotional, there would be reprisals, etc. YOU need to talk to Suzy...but please don't mention my name."

You've been there before, and you know what will happen if you talk to Suzy and tell her that someone has complained about her rudeness. With hands on hips and in a sarcastic voice, she'll say, "You've been talking to Sam. Right? He's always complaining about me. He doesn't like the fact that I have more seniority and get the better shifts. He's always trying to get me in trouble." Now you're in a no-win he said, she said situation. You can't placate one employee without making the other angry. Remember, getting in the middle of a triangulated conversation—even when you're the boss—is a doomed scenario.

Instead of talking to Suzy on Sam's behalf, your best option is to coach Sam on how to have the conversation with Suzy himself. Together, you can discuss which conversational model is best suited to the situation and what Sam should say to Suzy. You can even offer to play Suzy's role and practice with Sam until he feels more confident.

Now, let's examine a few variations of the Suzy/Sam scenario. Your advice to Sam will vary based on his role in the organization and his relationship to Suzy.

Scenario 1: Suzy and Sam are coworkers (but not leaders). If Suzy and Sam are coworkers in the same unit or department, Sam should have a Stub Your Toe Conversation with Suzy the next time he sees her displaying an undesirable behavior. If you cascade Stub Your Toe Conversations to your entire team and give them the opportunity to practice scenarios regularly, I think you'll find yourself playing "playground monitor" much less frequently.

Scenario 2: Suzy and Sam are both leaders in the organization. Here, suggest that Sam schedule some time for an Impact Message Conversation with Suzy. He should prepare specific examples of how Suzy's behavior is negatively impacting employee engagement/patient safety/patient satisfaction.

Scenario 3: Suzy has violated a policy or standard that requires immediate discipline. While it's usually best to encourage others to address grievances between themselves, there may be times you need to step in immediately. If Sam comes to you and indicates that Suzy has been drinking, doing drugs, or stealing, you need to get involved. If Suzy has been making sexual innuendos, using racial slurs, or threatening violence, you need to get involved. Work with your HR partner and make sure you know—in advance—the most appropriate way to handle these types of situations.

And What About the Docs?

When one physician witnesses unacceptable behaviors from a colleague, they may not say anything because they don't think it's their place to chastise a colleague—or they just don't know how to start the conversation. So they come to you, expecting that as the chief medical officer, CEO, or operating room director, it's your job to stop the behavior—which you haven't even seen. The best response is for you to coach the provider who saw and heard the unacceptable interaction on how to have a Stub Your Toe

Conversation with the colleague. Maybe you'll need to role play the conversation. Encourage the provider to have the conversation and report back to you on the outcome—that's accountability.

Still not convinced that you're ready to have tough conversations? Or is an employee or colleague experiencing doubt along those same lines? Remember what I wrote at the end of this book's Introduction: If you keep the face of the patient or customer in front of you, you'll know that having a direct (albeit difficult) conversation is the right thing to do.

When we *don't* have these conversations, our patients or customers choose not to return, and they share their negative experiences with others in the community and on the Internet. Furthermore, employees who *are* demonstrating the right behaviors leave when they see others disregarding our standards, policies, or other "rules." And finally, think of yourself: Do you really want to stay hidden in your office because you are afraid to take the first step and talk to an employee, colleague, boss, or customer about something that is disruptive? I didn't think so!

APPENDIX:

WHAT OTHERS SAY ABOUT COMMUNICATIONS

O ther books can—and have!—been written on many of the ideas, skills, and tactics I have covered in this book. In this section, I've pulled together some of my favorite quotes on communication in hopes that you, too, may find the information useful. I have also included a list of recommended works by Dr. Alan Rosenstein, whose research on disruptive behaviors has been referred to several times throughout this book. Remember, the more you learn, the better equipped you'll be to successfully conduct difficult conversations.

Astute Observations from Other Authors

Successfully conducting difficult conversations is, at heart, based on having good communication skills. Here are some nuggets of wisdom from other authors:

From ***Be Quiet, Be Heard***[1] by Susan R. Glaser and Peter A. Glaser:

When communication goes awry, the result is often retreat. But communication abhors a vacuum and so this avoidance is filled with negative assumptions and ill will. If the silence is broken, it is too often packed with the relentless noise of people making their own points over and over again. One sad truth remains: No one is really listening to anyone else.

- Trust is not a prerequisite for communications; trust is a byproduct of communication.

- The trouble with letting sleeping dogs lie is that we have to keep stepping over them.

- To foster a culture where praise becomes a norm, we must make it acceptable to receive praise as well as to give it. Like all communication, gratitude is a two-way street.

From ***Crucial Conversations***[2] by Kerry Patterson, Joseph Grenny, Ron McMillan, and Al Switzler:

- Master your crucial conversations and you'll kick-start your career, strengthen your relationships, and improve your health. As you and others master high-stakes discussions, you'll also vitalize your organization and your community.

- Skilled people Start with Heart. That is, they begin high-risk discussions with the right motives, and they stay focused no matter what happens.

From *Crucial Confrontations*[3] by Kerry Patterson, Joseph Grenny, Ron McMillan, and Al Switzler:

- Our research has shown that most organizations are losing between 20 and 80 percent of their potential performance because of leaders' and employees' inability to step up to and master crucial confrontations.

- If the solution you're applying doesn't get you the results you really want, it's likely you're dealing with the wrong problem entirely.

- Make recognition such an informal, spontaneous, important, and common part of your corporate and family culture that formal celebrations will feel heartfelt rather than mechanical and obligatory. Make praise such a common part of your personal style that when you do enter into a crucial confrontation, you'll have built a safe, trusting, and respectful relationship.

From *Fierce Conversations: Achieving Success at Work & in Life, One Conversation at a Time*[4] by Susan Scott:

- Companies and marriages derail temporarily or permanently because people don't say what they are really thinking.

- The fundamental outcome of most communication is misunderstanding.

From *Start with Why: How Great Leaders Inspire Everyone to Take Action*[5] by Simon Sinek:

- Communication is not about Speaking; it's about Listening.

Dr. Alan Rosenstein's Research on Disruptive Behavior

Dr. Alan Rosenstein has done extensive research on disruptive behavior and its impact on healthcare organizations. His research has focused on physicians, nurses, pharmacists, administrators, and other healthcare professionals as the initiators and recipients of disruptive behavior. Dr. Rosenstein's research documents that dysfunctional actions can impact quality of care, mortality, and employee engagement and turnover. The topic is a critical one that must be addressed in every organization seeking excellence.

The following sources will familiarize you with Dr. Rosenstein's work. They'll also help you start applying his findings to your organization:

- "Conflict Resolution: Unlocking the Key to Success," *Nursing Management.*[6]

- "Improving Physician Communication Efficiency: Wants, Needs, and Strategies," *Successful Nurse Communication: Safe Care, Positive Workplaces, and Rewarding Careers.*[7]

- "The Clinical Quality Challenge: The Importance of Physician Communication," *HealthLeaders.*[8]

- "Improving Physician Satisfaction and Care Management Efficiencies," *Becker's Hospital Review*.[9]

- "Addressing Disruptive Behaviors in Medicine: Opportunities for Improvement," *The Workplace Violence Prevention eReport*.[10]

- "The Impact of Physician Burnout," *Joint Commission Physician Blog*.[11]

ACKNOWLEDGMENTS

Merriam-Webster defines gratitude as "a feeling of appreciation or thanks." To feel grateful is to feel thankful for something. I cannot express enough how thankful I am for the many opportunities and experiences I have had throughout my professional and personal years. I am honored to share some of the things I have learned along the way throughout the pages of this book.

There have been many people in the course of my life who have provided inspiration, provided challenges (which of course helped me in developing some of these best practices), and provided help when needed. This book would not have been possible without the help of the following people:

To Quint Studer: Thank you for the years of coaching. It has been a pleasure working alongside someone with so much passion and purpose. You are truly a fire starter for thousands in healthcare and continue to make a difference.

To Craig Deao: Thanks for being such an incredible leader and trusted advisor for me as we travel the country speaking.

You are another difference maker, and I am honored to work alongside you.

To Jeff Morris, MD, Pam Saltenberger, Juli Miller, and Lynne Thomas Gordon: Thanks for your insight and review of early drafts of specific chapters.

To Bekki Kennedy: Thank you for believing in me and believing in this book. From the start, you helped to bring my most valuable experiences and research together to put forth the best book possible.

To Dottie DeHart & Company: Thanks to you and your team for taking my manuscript and helping get it to a final book that will be a valuable resource for readers.

To Melanie Carpenter: Thank you for being such a pillar at work that I can count on. Your support helps make my life a bit easier every day.

To Lindy Sikes and Jamie Stewart: Thanks for all your help in pulling together the many pieces and adding the final touches to get my book off to print and in the hands of those who will benefit from it.

To Lauren Westwood: Thank you for your ability to bring the graphics and charts in this book to life in order to enhance learning. Your attention to detail is amazing.

REFERENCES

Introduction:

1. Valcour, Monique. "How to Give Tough Feedback That Helps People Grow," *Harvard Business Review* (2015) https://hbr.org/2015/08/how-to-give-tough-feedback-that-helps-people-grow.

2. Ibid.

Chapter 3:

1. Rosenstein, Alan H. "Measuring and Managing the Economic Impact of Disruptive Behaviors in the Hospital," *Journal of Healthcare Risk Management* 30 (2010): 20-26. doi: 10.1002/jhrm.20049.

Chapter 4:

1. Mayer, Thom A. and Robert J. Cates. *Leadership for Great Customer Service.* Chicago: Health Administration Press, 2014.

Chapter 7:

1. Connellan, Tom. *Inside the Magic Kingdom*. London: Peak Performance, 1997.

2. Zenger, Jack and Joseph Folkman. "The Ideal Praise-to-Criticism Ratio," *Harvard Business Review* (2013) https://hbr.org/2013/03/the-ideal-praise-to-criticism

3. Ibid.

4. Graham, Gerald H. and Jeanne Unruh, "The Motivational Impact of Nonfinancial Employee Appreciation Practices on Medical Technologists," *Health Care Supervisor* 8 (2015): 9-17.

5. Rath, Tom and Donald Clifton. *How Full Is Your Bucket*. Washington D.C.: Gallup Press, 2004.

Chapter 11:

1. Lutgen-Sandvik, Pamela and Tracy, Sarah J., & Alberts, Jess K. "Burned by Bullying in the American Workplace: Prevalence, Perception, Degree, and Impact," *Journal of Management Studies* 44 (2007): 837-857, doi: 10.1111/j.1467-6486.2007.00715.x.

2. Boulanger, Amy. "Physical Effects of Workplace Aggression: The Toll Bullying Takes on Your Mind and Body," *Medical Daily* (2013) http://www.medicaldaily.com/physical-effects-workplace-aggression-toll-bullying-takes-your-mind-and-body-247018.

3. Holloway, Elizabeth L and Mitchell E. Kusy. "Toxic workers put organizations at risk," *Modern Healthcare*, August 4, 2014, http://www.modernhealthcare.com/article/20140802/MAGAZINE/308029979.

4. Boulanger, Amy. "Physical Effects of Workplace Aggression: The Toll Bullying Takes on Your Mind and Body," *Medical Daily* (2013) http://www.medicaldaily.com/physical-effects-workplace-aggression-toll-bullying-takes-your-mind-and-body-247018.

5. Rosenstein, Alan H. "Bad Medicine," *Risk Management* December (2013): 38-42.

6. Rosenstein, Alan H. "Physician Communication and Care Management: The Good, the Bad and the Ugly," *Physician Executive Journal* 38 (2012): 34-37.

7. Girl Scouts Research Institute. "The Bullying Problem," *GSRI E-Newsletter* 15 (2012).

8. Boulanger, Amy. "Physical Effects of Workplace Aggression: the Toll Bullying Takes on Your Mind and Body," *Medical Daily* (2013) http://www.medicaldaily.com/physical-effects-workplace-aggression-toll-bullying-takes-your-mind-and-body-247018.

9. Makary, Marty. *Unaccountable: What Hospitals Won't Tell You and How Transparency Can Revolutionize Health Care.* New York: Bloomsbury Press, 2012.

Appendix:

1. Glaser, Susan R. and Peter A. Glaser. *Be Quiet, Be Heard.* Communications Solutions Publishing, 2006.

2. Patterson, Kerry, Joseph Grenny, Ron McMillan, and Al Switzer. *Crucial Conversations.* New York: McGraw-Hill, 2002.

3. Patterson, Kerry, Joseph Grenny, Ron McMillan, and Al Switzer. *Crucial Confrontations*. New York: McGraw-Hill, 2004.

4. Scott, Susan. *Fierce Conversations: Achieving Success at Work and in Life, One Conversation at a Time*. New York: Berkley Books, 2002.

5. Sinek, Simon. *Start with Why: How Great Leaders Inspire Everyone to Take Action*. New York: Portfolio/Penguin, 2009.

6. Rosenstein, Alan H., Steven P. Dinkin, and James Munro. "Conflict resolution: Unlocking the key to success" *Nursing Management* 45 no.10 (2014): 34-39 doi: 10.1097/01. NUMA.0000454027.46483.4f

7. Rosenstein, Alan H. "Improving Physician Communication Efficiency: Wants, Needs, and Strategies" in *Successful Nurse Communication: Safe Care, Positive Workplaces, and Rewarding Careers*, 93-95. Philadelphia: F.A. Davis, 2015.

8. Rosenstein, Alan H. "The Clinical Quality Challenge: The Importance of Physician Communication" *Health-Leaders* 17 no. 6 (2014): 8.

9. Rosenstein, Alan H. "Improving Physician Satisfaction and Care Management Efficiencies" *Becker's Hospital Review* (2014). http://www.beckershospitalreview.com/hospital-physician-relationships/improving-physician-satisfaction-and-care-management-efficiencies.html

10. Rosenstein, Alan H. "Addressing Disruptive Behaviors in Medicine: Opportunities for Improvement" *The Workplace Violence Prevention eReport* 10 (2014): 14-15. http://content.yudu.com/Library/A36svk/TheWorkplaceViolence/?refid=74211

11. Rosenstein, Alan H. and Michael R. Privitera. "The Impact of Physician Burnout" *Leadership* (blog), Joint Commission, January 28, 2015, http://www.jointcommission.org/jc_physician_blog/the_impact_of_physician_burnout/

Additional Resources

ABOUT STUDER GROUP®, A HURON HEALTHCARE SOLUTION:

Learn more about Studer Group® by scanning the QR code with your mobile device or by visiting www.studergroup.com/who-we-are/about-studer-group.

Studer Group works with healthcare organizations in the United States, Canada, Australia, and beyond to help them achieve and sustain exceptional improvement in clinical outcomes and financial results. A Huron Healthcare solution, Studer Group partners with organizations to build a sustainable culture that promotes accountability, fosters innovation, and consistently delivers a great patient experience and the best quality outcomes over time. By installing an execution framework called Evidence-Based Leadership[SM] (EBL), organizations are able to align goals, actions, and processes and execute quickly. This framework creates the foundation that enables transformation in this era of continuous change.

To learn more about partnering with Studer Group on your journey to improvement, visit www.studergroup.com or call 850-439-5839.

STUDER GROUP COACHING:

Learn more about Studer Group coaching by scanning the QR code with your mobile device or by visiting www.studergroup.com/coaching.

Studer Group coaches partner with healthcare organizations to create an aligned culture accountable for achieving outcomes together. Working side-by-side, we help to establish, accelerate, and hardwire the necessary changes to create a culture of excellence. This leads to better transparency, higher accountability, and the ability to target and execute specific, objective results that organizations want to achieve. Studer Group offers specialized coaching based on organizational needs: Evidence-Based Leadership Coaching, System Coaching, Emergency Department Coaching, Physician Coaching, Medical Practice Coaching, and Rural Coaching.

BOOKS: CATEGORIZED BY AUDIENCE

Explore the Fire Starter Publishing website by scanning the QR code with your mobile device or by visiting www.fire-starterpublishing.com.

Senior Leaders & Physicians

A Culture of High Performance: Achieving Higher Quality at a Lower Cost—A must-have book for any leader struggling to shore up margins while sustaining an organization that is a great place for employees to work, physicians to practice medicine, and patients to receive care. From best-selling author Quint Studer to help you build a culture that will thrive during change.

Straight A Leadership: Alignment, Action, Accountability—A guide that will help you identify gaps in alignment, action, and accountability; create a plan to fill them; and become a more resourceful, agile, high-performing organization, written by Quint Studer.

Engaging Physicians: A Manual to Physician Partnership—A tactical and passionate road map for physician collaboration to generate organizational high performance, written by Stephen C. Beeson, MD.

Healing Physician Burnout: Diagnosing, Preventing, and Treating—Written by Quint Studer, in collaboration with George Ford, MD, this book helps leaders and physicians work together to create healthy environments for practicing medicine while navigating the huge changes disrupting our industry. It explores why physicians are so burned out and provides practical tools to get them engaged, aligned, and reconnected to their sense of meaning and purpose.

Excellence with an Edge: Practicing Medicine in a Competitive Environment—An insightful book that provides practical tools and techniques you need to know to have a solid grasp of the business side of making a living in healthcare, written by Michael T. Harris, MD.

Physicians

The CG CAHPS Handbook: A Guide to Improve Patient Experience and Clinical Outcomes—Written by Jeff Morris, MD, MBA, FACS; Barbara Hotko, RN, MPA; and Matthew Bates, MPH. *The CG CAHPS Handbook* is your guide for consistently delivering on what matters most to patients and their families and for providing exceptional care and improved clinical outcomes.

Practicing Excellence: A Physician's Manual to Exceptional Health Care—This book, written by Stephen C. Beeson, MD, is a brilliant guide to implementing physician leadership and behaviors that will create a high-performance workplace.

All Leaders

101 Answers to Questions Leaders Ask—By Quint Studer and Studer Group coaches, offers practical, prescriptive solutions from healthcare leaders around the country.

Eat That Cookie!: Make Workplace Positivity Pay Off...For Individuals, Teams, and Organizations—Written by Liz Jazwiec, RN, this book is funny, inspiring, relatable, and is packed with realistic, down-to-earth tactics to infuse positivity into your culture.

Hardwiring Excellence—A *BusinessWeek* bestseller, this book is a road map to creating and sustaining a "Culture of Service and Operational Excellence" that drives bottom-line results. Written by Quint Studer.

Hey Cupcake! We Are ALL Leaders—Author Liz Jazwiec explains that we'll all eventually be called on to lead someone, whether it's a department, a shift, a project team, or a new employee. In her trademark slightly sarcastic (and hilarious) voice, she provides learned-the-hard-way insights that will benefit leaders in every industry and at every level.

"I'm Sorry to Hear That..." Real-Life Responses to Patients' 101 Most Common Complaints About Health Care—When you respond to a patient's complaint, you are responding to the patient's sense of helplessness and anxiety. The service recovery scripts offered in this book can help you recover a patient's confidence in you and your organization. Authored by Susan Keane Baker and Leslie Bank.

Oh No...Not More of That Fluffy Stuff! The Power of Engagement—Written by Rich Bluni, RN, this funny, heartfelt book explores what it takes to overcome obstacles and tap into the passion that fuels our best work. Its practical exercises help employees at all levels get happier, more excited, and more connected to the meaning in our daily lives.

Over Our Heads: An Analogy on Healthcare, Good Intentions, and Unforeseen Consequences— This book, written by Rulon F. Stacey, PhD, FACHE, uses a grocery store analogy to illustrate how government intervention leads to economic crisis and, eventually, collapse.

Results That Last: Hardwiring Behaviors That Will Take Your Company to the Top—A *Wall Street Journal* bestseller by Quint Studer that teaches leaders in every industry how to apply his tactics and strategies to their own organizations to build a corporate culture that consistently reaches and exceeds its goals.

Service Excellence Is As Easy As PIE (Perception Is Everything)— Realistic, down to earth, and wickedly witty, *PIE* is perfect for everyone in healthcare or any other service industry. It's filled with ideas for creating exceptional customer experiences— ideas that are surprising, simple, and yes, easy as you-know-what. Written by Liz Jazwiec.

The Great Employee Handbook: Making Work and Life Better— This book is a valuable resource for employees at all levels who want to learn how to handle tough workplace situations—skills that normally come only from a lifetime of experience. *Wall Street Journal* best-selling author Quint Studer has pulled together the best insights gained from working with thousands of employees during his career.

Nurse Leaders and Nurses

Inspired Nurse and *Inspired Journal*—By Rich Bluni, RN. Help maintain and recapture the inspiration nurses felt at the start of their journey with action-oriented "spiritual stretches" and stories that illuminate those sacred moments we all experience.

The HCAHPS Handbook, 2nd Edition: Tactics to Improve Quality and the Patient Experience—Revised and released in 2015, this book is a valuable resource for organizations seeking to provide the exceptional quality of care their patients expect and deserve. Coauthored by Lyn Ketelsen, RN, MBA; Karen Cook, RN; and Bekki Kennedy.

The Nurse Leader Handbook: The Art and Science of Nurse Leadership—By Studer Group senior nursing and physician leaders from across the country, is filled with knowledge that provides nurse leaders with a solid foundation for success. It also serves as a reference they can revisit again and again when they have questions or need a quick refresher course in a particular area of the job.

Emergency Department Team

Advance Your Emergency Department: Leading in a New Era—As this critical book asserts, world-class Emergency Departments don't follow. They lead. Stephanie J. Baker, RN, CEN, MBA; Regina Shupe, RN, MSN, CEN; and Dan Smith, MD, FACEP, share high-impact strategies and tactics to help your ED get results more efficiently, effectively, and collaboratively. Master them and you'll improve quality, exceed patient expectations, and ultimately help the entire organization maintain and grow its profit margin.

Excellence in the Emergency Department: How to Get Results—A book by Stephanie Baker, RN, CEN, MBA, is filled with proven, easy-to-implement, step-by-step instructions that will help you move your Emergency Department forward.

Hardwiring Flow: Systems and Processes for Seamless Patient Care—Drs. Thom Mayer and Kirk Jensen delve into one of the most critical issues facing healthcare leaders: patient flow.

The Patient Flow Advantage: How Hardwiring Hospital-Wide Flow Drives Competitive Performance—Build effectiveness, efficiency, and a patient-centric focus into the heart of every process that serves the patient. Efficient patient flow has never been more critical to ensure patient safety, satisfaction, and optimal reimbursement. Authored by Drs. Kirk Jensen and Thom Mayer.

STUDER CONFERENCES:

Learn more about Studer Group conferences by scanning the QR code with your mobile device or by visiting www.studergroup.com/conferences.

Studer Conferences are three-day interactive learning events designed to provide healthcare leaders with an authentic, practical learning experience. Each Studer Conference includes internationally renowned keynote speakers and tracks concentrated on key areas of the healthcare organization. Every track includes breakout sessions and "how-to" workshops that provide you with direct access to experts and conference faculty. The faculty at Studer Conferences go beyond Power-Point slides and lectures to show you "what right looks like."

Leaders will leave with new tools and skills that get results. Find out more about upcoming Studer Conferences and register at www.studergroup.com/conferences.

All Studer Group Conferences offer Continuing Education Credits. For more information on CMEs, visit www.studergroup.com/cmecredits.

STUDER SPEAKING:

Learn more about Studer Group conferences by scanning the QR code with your mobile device or by visiting www.studergroup.com/speaking.

From large association events to exclusive executive training, Studer Group speakers deliver the perfect balance of inspiration and education for every audience. As experienced clinicians and administrators, each speaker has a unique journey to share. This personal touch, along with hard-hitting healthcare improvement tactics, empowers your team to take action and to drive organizational growth with training that reaches leaders at all levels.

ABOUT THE AUTHOR

Lynne Cunningham is an internationally renowned speaker, coach, and author. A leader in healthcare communication, she has over four decades in the industry. Besides *Taking Conversations from Difficult to Doable*, she has written several other books, including *The Future of Health Care Marketing, Public Relations, and Communications* and *The Quality Connection in Health Care*. Lynne has also authored many journal articles on topics like patient satisfaction and physician partnership.

She was a staff administrator at Kaiser Permanente in Northern California and a vice president overseeing communications and marketing at Sutter Health. She also founded Cunningham Associates, a consulting practice specializing in qualitative research and strategic planning for healthcare organizations throughout the U.S. Joining Studer Group® in 1999, Lynne is currently a coach and speaker. She works with hospitals, health systems, and medical groups all over the country to define, measure, and evaluate the perception of quality among patients, employees, physicians, and the community.

Lynne earned a bachelor of science from Northern Arizona University and a master of public administration (MPA) from California State University. She is a fellow of the American College of Healthcare Executives.

She resides in California with Glen, her husband of over 45 years. When Lynne is not speaking, she and Glen enjoy hiking, cross-country skiing, and international travel.

How to Order Additional Copies of

Taking Conversations from Difficult to Doable

Orders may be placed:

Online at: www.firestarterpublishing.com/difficulttodoable

Scan the QR code with your mobile device to order through the Fire Starter Publishing website.

By phone at: 866-354-3473

By mail at: Fire Starter Publishing
350 W. Cedar Street, Suite 300
Pensacola, FL 32502

Share this book with your team—and save!
Taking Conversations from Difficult to Doable is filled with valuable information. If purchasing for a team, please contact Fire Starter Publishing at 866-354-3473 to learn more about potential bulk savings.

Book Lynne Cunningham for your next training event.
Take your speaking event to the next level by having Lynne live and in person at your next session. A skilled facilitator with keen insight into group dynamics, Lynne is able to work individually with organizations to help them determine the best way to apply and integrate Studer Group processes as they create their own "fingerprint" for their cultural change journey. Visit www.studergroup.com/speaking to learn how you can request Lynne to speak at your organization.